Riding

MW01016980

SOUTHWEST
WASHINGTON
Horse Trails

By Kim McCarrel

Happy Trails!
Kim McCarrel

Over 100 Trails to Explore on Horseback
20 Horse Camps
Over 1,000 Miles of Trails

Ponderosa Press
Bend, Oregon

Riding Southwest Washington Horse Trails
1st Edition 2016
2nd Edition 2018

ON THE COVER:
Mt. Adams from the Muddy Meadows Trail near Keenes Horse Camp

AT RIGHT:
Goat Rocks Wilderness from the Pacific Crest Trail
near White Pass Horse Camp

Published by

Ponderosa Press

64495 Old Bend Redmond Hwy., Bend, OR 97703
www.NWHorseTrails.com
Copyright 2018
ISBN 978-0-9826770-4-9

Safety Notice: Every effort has been made to ensure that the information in this guidebook is as accurate as possible at press time. However, horseback riding is an inherently dangerous activity, and you are responsible for your own safety on the trails. Ponderosa Press and the author are not responsible for any loss, damage, or injury that may occur to anyone using this book. The information contained in this guidebook cannot replace good judgment. The fact that a trail is described in this book does not mean it will be safe for you. Trail conditions can change from day to day, so always check local conditions and know your own limitations.

The world is best viewed through the ears of a horse.

Anonymous

4

Contents

Maps

When you're riding, always carry with you a detailed map of the area.
The best maps for the trails in SW Washington are:

Gifford Pinchot National Forest Map
Cowlitz Valley Ranger District Map
Mt. Adams Ranger District Map
Goat Rocks Wilderness Map
Indian Heaven Wilderness Map
Mt. St. Helens National Volcanic Monument Map
William O. Douglas Wilderness Map
Capitol State Forest Map
Elbe/Tahoma State Forest Map

Printable maps for state parks are available at
http://parks.state.wa.us/432/Park-maps.
Washington Competitive Mounted Orienteering has a variety of
excellent printable maps at http://wacmo.org/maps/.
Various other riding areas have printable maps online.

Mt. Adams from Muddy Meadows Trail, near Keenes Horse Camp.

Foreword

Ride through old-growth forests, past cascading waterfalls, and beside burbling streams. Experience the stark beauty of the Columbia Gorge. Take in the panoramic views from the flanks of volcanic peaks. It's all here, and much more, in Southwest Washington.

This book covers the area from Olympia south to the Columbia River, and from the coast to the crest of the Cascade Mountains. The trails range from easy bridle paths to challenging wilderness single-tracks. You'll find everything from sandy beaches and rolling hills to dense forests, waterfalls, alpine lakes, and mountain vistas. And in spring and early summer the wildflower displays are spectacular.

The purpose of this guidebook is to provide the information you need to decide whether a particular trail is right for you: what the terrain is like, how difficult the ride is, how to find the trailhead, and what facilities you will find when you get there. We hope this book encourages you to try out some trails you haven't ridden yet.

The information provided here is as accurate as possible as of its publication date. But of course, conditions change over time so we've included information on how to contact local land managers for updated conditions.

See you on the trails!

Kim McCarrel

Mt. St. Helens from the Goat Mountain Trail.

Southwest Washington Horse Trails

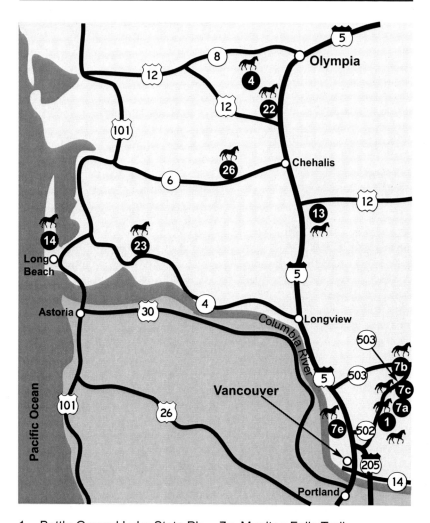

1. Battle Ground Lake State Pk.
2. Beacon Rock State Park
3. Brooks Memorial State Park
4. Capitol State Forest
5. Cody Horse Camp
6a. Buck Creek Trail
6b. Catherine Creek
6c. Columbia Hills State Park
6d. Klickitat Trail

7a. Moulton Falls Trail
7b. Saddle Dam Area
7c. Siouxon Creek Trail
7d. Washougal Dike
7e. Whipple Creek Trail
8. Falls Creek Horse Camp
9. Grayback Mountain
10. Green River Horse Camp
11. Kalama Horse Camp

Southwest Washington Horse Trails

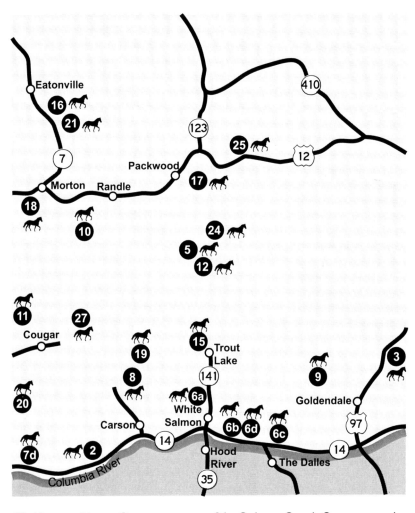

12. Keenes Horse Camp
13. Lewis & Clark State Park
14. Long Beach
15. Mt. Adams Horse Camp
16. Pack Forest
17. Packwood Lake
18. Peterman Hill
19. Placid Lake
20. Rock Creek Campground

21. Sahara Creek Campground
22. Scatter Creek
23. Tunerville Campground
24. Walupt Horse Camp
25. White Pass Horse Camp
26. Willapa Hills Trail
27. Wright Meadow

Saddlebag Savvy

The difference between a great ride and a lousy one, or between a mild misadventure and a disaster, may hinge upon whether you brought along the proper gear. Even on a short ride, it's a good idea to carry the "Ten Essentials" for survival, and know how to use them.

1. Navigation: Always carry a map of the area you'll be riding, even if you know the trail. Carry a compass and/or GPS and know how to use it. And of course, extra batteries for your GPS are a must.

2. Water: You can live for weeks without food, but only a few days without water. Carry extra water, along with water purification tablets or a water purifier just in case.

3. Extra Clothing: Always bring one more layer of clothing than you think you'll need. Rain gear, a hat, and gloves are the most important items, and an extra fleece jacket is a good idea. Extra packets of hand and toe warmers are easy to carry, and an emergency space blanket takes up little room but you'll be glad you have it if you have to spend a night on the trail.

4. Food: Bring along food for one more meal than you think you'll need. Trail mix, energy bars, dried fruit, and other snacks are good items to have on hand. A neat trick is to keep a can of tuna in your saddle bag. You won't be tempted to snack on it during a normal ride and it will keep forever, so if an emergency occurs and you need it, it will be there.

5. Light: If you have to spend the night on the trail, you'll be glad to have a flashlight and extra batteries on hand. A flashlight also comes in handy for signaling. Don't store the flashlight with the batteries inside, in case the flashlight gets accidentally switched on and drains the batteries. A headlamp is nice for keeping your hands free.

6. Fire: Waterproof matches and a fire starter like a candle stub can make a night stranded on the mountain a lot more comfortable.

7. Sun Protection: Sunglasses and extra sunscreen may not seem like survival essentials, but the lack of them can sure make your trip less enjoyable. Sunscreen needs to be reapplied occasionally for optimal effectiveness, so bring some extra along.

8. First Aid: Any Scout worth his or her salt knows you should carry a first aid kit. Equestrians should carry first aid items for people (bandaids, insect repellent, insect bite cream, antibiotic ointment, gauze pads, adhesive tape, a needle for removing splinters, ace bandage, small scissors, personal prescriptions, etc.) as well as first aid items for horses (vet wrap, equine thermometer, antiseptic scrub, Banamine, etc.) Be sure someone in your party has had training in first aid.

9. Knife: A good knife is essential, since it can help with fire building, first aid, and food preparation. A Leatherman-type tool will include other helpful gadgets in addition to a knife, like saws, tweezers, screwdrivers, scissors, can opener, etc.

10. Signal: With a cell phone and a fully-charged battery, you may be able to summon help in an emergency. However, cell coverage is not reliable, especially in the wilderness. A loud whistle and a metal signaling mirror can help rescuers find you faster. Three blasts or flashes mean "help needed." A Spot emergency locator beacon is a good idea, and walkie-talkies can help keep a group in contact if you get separated.

Bonus Ideas: It goes without saying that wearing a helmet may save your life. Other things that can come in very handy in a trail emergency include a large plastic garbage bag (can be used as a poncho, a tent, a ground cloth, or to carry water) and twine or a shoelace for tack

Long Beach

Saddlebag Savvy (cont.)

repairs. Put your contact information in your saddle bag in case your horse gets loose and runs off. And be sure to carry your important medical information on your person (in your pocket, or tucked inside the inner rim of your helmet) in case you get hurt and are unconscious when paramedics arrive.

It's also important to consider which items should be on your person instead of in your saddlebag. Waterproof matches, your cell phone, and a knife are probably the bare minimum. If you and your horse get separated, all that great emergency equipment in your saddlebag won't do you any good. If your riding clothes are short on pockets, use a fanny pack or a Cashel Ankle Safe trail pouch to carry critical items.

Finally, always tell someone where you are going and when you'll be returning, then stick with your plan. That way if something goes wrong, they'll know where to start looking for you.

Ride safely, be prepared, and have fun!

Columbia Hills State Park

Certified Feed Required

To help control the spread of invasive species in the Northwest, both the Forest Service and the Bureau of Land Management now require that any horse feed brought onto Federal land must be certified to be free of weed seeds.

The Forest Service's catchy name for this special horse feed is "Weed Seed-Free Feed." (Say that three times fast!) Most folks call it "certified feed" instead.

There are two types of certified feed: hay that a state agricultural inspector has deemed to be free of weed seeds, or heat-processed feed pellets. (The heat treatment kills the seeds and prevents them from germinating.)

The bottom line for horseback riders is that if you go on Federal land, you are allowed to have only certified feed in your trailer or at your campsite. If you violate this requirement, you can be ticketed and fined.

You can purchase certified hay or pellets from most feed stores, or go to http://agr.wa.gov/PlantsInsects/WWHAM/docs/WWHAMCertifiedGrowers.pdf for a list of certified hay producers.

Packwood Lake Trail

Leave No Trace Principles

Leave No Trace is a nationally-recognized outdoor skills and ethics education program. Its seven Leave No Trace Principles outline the ways that recreational users can minimize the impact we have on the land. The principles are listed below, followed by specific things we equestrians can do to ensure that the beautiful places we enjoy today will be preserved for generations to come.

Plan Ahead and Prepare
-- Educate yourself about the area you plan to visit. Talk with local land managers to find out about trail conditions. Know before you go.
-- Carry and use a map, and take responsibility for knowing your route and staying on it.
-- Tell someone where you are going, and stick with your itinerary.

Travel and Camp on Durable Surfaces
-- Water your horse directly from a stream or lake only at trail crossings or if there is a rocky or sandy bank. Otherwise, bring water to your horse using a collapsible bucket to protect fragile shoreline vegetation.
-- Above the tree line, please stay on the trails to avoid damaging fragile alpine environments.
-- Use trails designated for horse use.
-- When traveling cross-country, don't ride single file. Each rider should pick his own route to disperse hoofprints, staying on durable surfaces.
-- Avoid steep slopes and soft ground. Ride across slopes rather than straight up or down to reduce erosion.
-- To minimize damage, don't ride trails that are wet and muddy.

Dispose of Waste Properly
-- Pack out all garbage.
-- Disburse any manure piles after rest breaks on the trail.
-- When you stop for a bathroom break, make sure you're at least 200 feet (that's about 75 steps) away from any streams, lakes, or springs. Bury all waste, and carry out your used toilet paper.

Leave What You Find
-- Use certified feed to help prevent the spread of invasive species. Start feeding it to your animals three or more days before entering the forest so their digestive systems are clear of weed seeds.
-- Fill in pawed ground to help the vegetation regrow.
-- Do not allow horses to paw or chew vegetation.

Minimize Campfire Impacts
-- Build fires only if the weather is safe, and use only dead and downed wood that is smaller than your wrist. Make sure your campfire is dead out before leaving it.

Respect Wildlife
-- Control your dog. Electronic collars work well on the trail.

Be Considerate of Other Visitors
-- Please keep horses out of lakes in the wilderness, as these lakes are used for drinking water by backpackers.
-- Keep horses off designated bike trails. Horse hooves break up the firm trail tread that bicyclists enjoy.
-- If you encounter hikers that are not familiar with horse traffic, greet them and ask them to move off to the downhill side of the trail, and coach them as needed.
-- A friendly equestrian makes a lasting impression on other trail users.

For more information about Leave No Trace principles, go to www.lnt.org/programs/ principles.php.

Mt. Adams from the Klickitat Wildlife Area, near Grayback Mountain

Pacific waterleaf

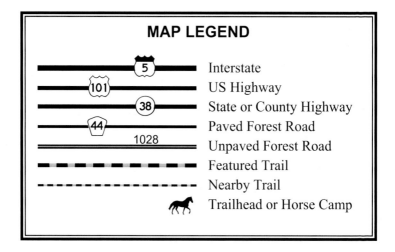

Battle Ground Lake State Park

Washington State Parks

Back in 1855, settlers at Fort Vancouver expected a battle between the US Army and local Klickitat Indians near what today we call Battle Ground Lake. The battle didn't occur, but the name for the area stuck. Battle Ground Lake itself lies within a volcanic caldera and is believed to be a miniature version of Oregon's Crater Lake.

At Battle Ground Lake State Park you'll find over 5 miles of equestrian trails that are open year-round, and a semi-primitive horse camp that's available by reservation.

The horse trails don't offer a view of Battle Ground Lake, but if you take the spur trail to Marshall Lookout you can tie your horse and walk a short distance to a viewpoint with this filtered view of the lake below.

Getting to Battle Ground Lake

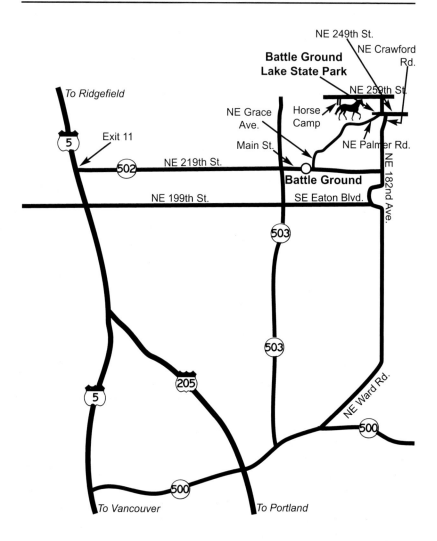

Battle Ground Lake Trails

Trail	Difficulty	Elevation	Round Trip
Battle Ground Lake Horse Trail	Easy	450-700	5 miles

Battle Ground Lake Horse Camp

Directions to:

Day-Use: From I-5, take the Battle Ground exit (Exit 11) and head east on NE 219th St (Hwy. 502). In about 6 miles you'll cross Hwy. 503 and the road will become Main St. as you enter downtown Battle Ground. Continue straight ahead for 3.0 miles and turn left on NE 182nd Ave. After 1.1 miles the road bends a little and becomes NE Crawford Rd. In 0.3 mile turn left on NE 249th St. Drive 0.1 mile to the junction with NE Palmer Road and NE 182nd Ave. Continue straight ahead to enter the park. In 500 feet turn left into the trailer parking area.

Camping: The campground is on the northwest corner of the park, off NE 259th St. Follow the directions above but instead of entering the park as above, turn right on NE 182nd Ave. Drive 0.5 mile and turn left on NE 259th St. In 0.6 mile, turn left again on the gated dirt road that leads to the horse camp.

Elevation: 550 feet

Campsites: The horse camp is available by reservation only. Four sites each have a 2-horse corral, barbecue pit, & picnic table. All sites are pull-throughs, though only 2 are level. Room for 2 trailers at 3 of the sites.

Facilities: The campground has a toilet, potable water from a spigot, manure bins, and garbage cans. The day-use area has parking for 10-15 horse trailers (depending on where hiker cars are parked), plus a toilet, manure bin, and garbage cans.

Permits: Discover Pass required for day-use parking. Fee for overnight camping.

Season: Year round, though trails can be quite muddy after rain

Contact: Battle Ground Lake State Park, 360-687-4621. For camping reservations, call 888-226-7680.

Battle Ground Lake Horse Trails

Trailhead:	Start at the horse trailer parking area off NE 249th St. or the horse camp
Length:	About 5 miles of horse trails
Elevation:	450 to 700 feet
Difficulty:	Easy
Footing:	Hoof protection suggested
Season:	Year round, though the trails can be very muddy after rain
Permits:	Discover Pass for day use, or fee for overnight camping
Facilities:	Parking for 10-15 trailers at the day-use area, plus toilet and manure bin. No stock water on the trail.

Highlights: The horse trails circle the perimeter of the park, running under a dense canopy of Douglas-firs. Vine maples and alders grow

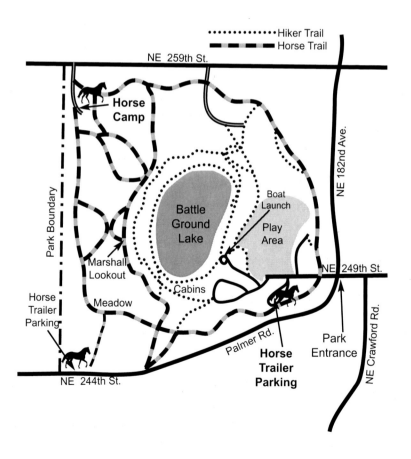

in the understory, providing spectacular color in autumn. Sword ferns, thimbleberries, and snowberries cover the ground. The beautiful forest is definitely the star of the show on these trails.

The Ride: The horse trail departs from the southwest and southeast ends of the main horse trailer parking area. On the east side of the park there is only one possible route, but on the west side you'll find several trails that make loops of various lengths as they travel up and down the low hills. In the southwest corner of the park, the trail goes through a meadow with an indistinct side trail that links to a second trailer-parking area. The perimeter trail is about 3 miles long, and you can add some mileage by exploring the other trails on the west side of the park. While the park advertises that its trails are open year round, in the winter and early spring the trails are too muddy to be enjoyable. The best seasons here are summer and fall.

Lisa rides Jane through the forest at Battle Ground Lake State Park.

Buttercup

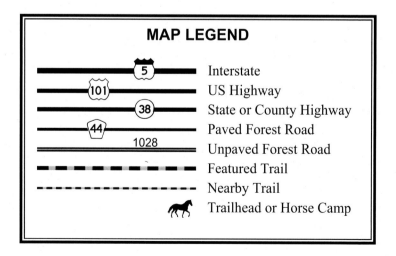

Beacon Rock State Park

Washington State Parks

When Lewis and Clark traveled down the Columbia in 1805, they spotted an 848-foot basalt monolith on the Washington side of the Columbia River near present-day Stevenson and named it Beacon Rock. In 1915 the rock was purchased by Henry Biddle, who built a highly-engineered trail to the summit. When Mr. Biddle died, the family offered Beacon Rock to the state of Washington for a park. Washington officials weren't interested -- until the state of Oregon offered to accept it. The Washington officials changed their minds, and Beacon Rock became a Washington state park in 1935. The park covers 5,100 acres that encompass Beacon Rock, Hardy Ridge, and Hamilton Mountain. The park has 13 miles of horse trails, all of which are also open to hikers and mountain bikes. The park also has a small horse camp for overnight visitors.

You'll find a panoramic view of the Columbia Gorge and Hamilton Mountain from the "Saddle Viewpoint" on the Equestrian Trail.

Getting to Beacon Rock

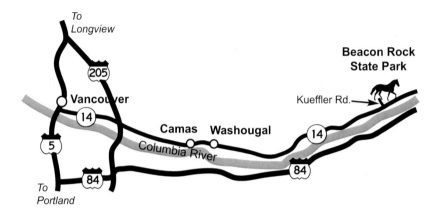

*Breeze enjoys her breakfast on the highline at the Beacon Rock
State Park equestrian trailhead and horse camp.*

Beacon Rock Horse Camp

Directions: From Washougal, drive east on Hwy. 14 for 18 miles. Turn left on Kueffler Road. In 1 mile, turn right at the sign for the equestrian trailhead and continue 0.4 mile to the horse camp and trailhead at the end of the road. Four-wheel drive recommended.

Elevation: 750 feet

Campsites: 2 back-in sites share a 90-foot highline with tie rings for 6 horses. Fire pits and picnic tables.

Facilities: Vault toilet, manure bins, garbage cans, stock water from a hand pump. Day-use parking for 10+ trailers.

Permits: Camping fee. Discover Pass required for day use.

Season: Mid-April through October

Contact: Washington State Parks, 509-427-8265

Beacon Rock State Park Trails

Trail	Difficulty	Elevation	Round Trip
Equestrian Tr. to Saddle Viewpoint	Easy	750-2,100	7 miles
West Hardy Ridge	Easy	750-2,250	5.5 miles
East Hardy Ridge	Easy	750-2,100	7 miles
Lower Loop Trail	Easy	750-1,600	4 miles
Equestrian/Upper Hardy Loop	Moderate	750-2,250	9 miles
Equestrian/Upper Hardy Creek/ Bridge/East Hardy Ridge Loop	Moderate	750-2,250	9 miles

Hamilton Mountain Trails

Trailhead: Start at the Beacon Rock State Park equestrian trailhead and horse camp

Length: Varies by route selected

Elevation: 750 to 2,250 feet

Difficulty: Easy trails, but the steady elevation gain means your horse will need to be in condition

Footing: Hoof protection a must

Season: Spring through fall

Permits: Discover Pass required

Facilities: Toilet, stock water from a pump, and manure bin at the horse camp/trailhead. Stock water is available on the trail.

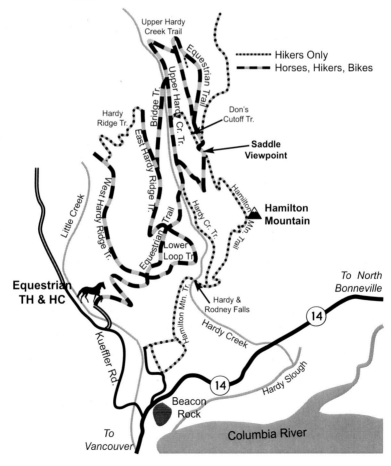

Highlights: The trails leading from the Beacon Rock equestrian trail-head and horse camp explore the slopes of Hamilton Mountain and Hardy Ridge. The Equestrian Trail runs along a gravel road that provides all-weather footing. The other trails are mostly single-tracks that run along the routes of old forests roads. The East and West Hardy Ridge Trails are out-and-back trails, or you can create several loops by connecting the Equestrian Trail with the Upper Hardy Creek Trail, the Bridge Trail, East Hardy Ridge Trail, and the Lower Loop Trail. The views from the Saddle Viewpoint and from upper Hardy Ridge are panoramic.

The Ride: The Equestrian Trail departs from the north end of the trail-head/camping area. It follows a single-track for a short distance, then veers onto a gravel forest road. In 1.2 miles the West Hardy Ridge Trail goes off to the left and the Lower Loop Trail goes to the right. From here it's 0.6 mile to the East Hardy Ridge Trail, 1.2 miles to the Hardy Creek Trail, 1.4 miles to the Upper Hardy Creek Trail, 2.5 miles to the Bridge Trail, and 2.3 miles to the Saddle Viewpoint.

The Equestrian Trail at Beacon Rock State Park runs on a gravel road that provides good footing even in wet weather.

Cow parsnip

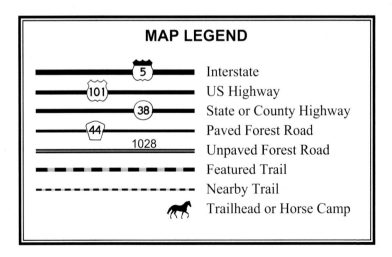

Brooks Memorial State Park

Washington State Parks

Brooks Memorial State Park lies in the transition zone between the south Yakima Valley and the pine-covered slopes of the Simcoe Mountains. This 70-year-old park used to have an extensive network of horse-friendly trails, but they fell into dis-use and became overgrown. Luckily, park managers have recently teamed up with Back Country Horsemen volunteers to re-open the trails in the park. A nine-mile network of horse trails now traverses the park's low hills, running through a mixed forest of ponderosa pine, oak, and Douglas-fir. You can also ride cross-country to explore the open hilltops of this 900-acre park. A horse camp is currently in the planning stages. Meanwhile, you can day-ride there at any time, and you can arrange to primitive camp at the park by reservation. Photocopied maps of the trails are available at the ranger station.

*Theresa rides Breeze through a meadow
at Brooks Memorial State Park.*

Getting to Brooks State Park

Breeze and Tex relax on their highline near where the planned horse camp at Brooks Memorial State Park may be built.

Brooks Park Equestrian Area

Directions: From Goldendale, take Hwy. 97 north for 11 miles. Directly across from the park's large entrance sign on the left, turn right on an unsigned road. Drive past the ranger station and a couple of staff houses, and when the road forks veer right (opening the gate if it is closed) toward the group camp. After 0.4 mile, turn right into an open area next to a stand of ponderosa pines and oaks. This area is currently available for equestrian day use and may be used for overnight camping if you make prior arrangements with park officials.

Elevation: 2,700 feet

Campsites: The horse camp is still in the planning phase, so facilities are limited. Meanwhile this area doubles as the park's equestrian parking area.

Facilities: Potable water from a spigot, picnic table, parking for 6-8 trailers, and trees for highlining. You'll find vault toilets at the group camp 0.2 mile farther down the road. If you cross Hwy. 97 and go to the family campground, you'll find coin-operated hot showers. The equestrian parking area is close to Hwy. 97, so road noise can be an issue.

Permits: Camping fee. Camping reservations required, 509-773-4611. Discover Pass required for day use.

Season: May through October

Contact: Brooks Memorial State Park, 509-773-4611

Brooks Park Area Trails

Trail	Difficulty	Elevation	Round Trip
Brooks Mem. State Park Trails	Moderate	2,500-3,000	Varies

Brooks Mem. State Park Trails

Trailhead: Start at the equestrian parking area at Brooks Memorial
State Park

Length: 9 miles of trail, plus there are forest roads to explore and
you can ride cross-country

Elevation: 2,500 to 3,000 feet

Difficulty: Moderate

Footing: Hoof protection recommended

Season: May through October

Permits: Camping fee, or Discover Pass for day use

Facilities: Potable water and picnic table at the equestrian parking
area. Toilets at the group camp 0.2 mile down the road.
No stock water on the trail.

Highlights: Volunteers from the Mt. Adams chapter of Back Country Horsemen have been working closely with park officials to re-build and sign the historic trails that explore the hills on the east side of Hwy. 97. The lower-elevation trails have been reconstructed and are well signed, allowing you to create several easy loops that run through an interesting forest of ponderosa pines, oaks, and Douglas-firs. One of these trails will take you to a forest road with a gate across it. You can go through the gate (please re-close it) and explore the park's hilltops, which are covered with stands of oaks and grassy meadows that offer views toward the Columbia Gorge. On the hilltops you can ride the

Theresa rides Breeze down the trail at Brooks Memorial State Park.

forest roads, follow the indistinct trails, or go cross-country. There's even a spot where you can see Mt. Hood.

The Ride: From the equestrian parking area, ride back toward the highway on the road you drove in on. When you reach the gate in 0.1 mile, go around it and turn right on the paved road toward the Environmental Learning Center (ELC). Follow the paved road for 0.2 mile and turn left on the first dirt road you come to. In 30 feet, turn either left or right to pick up the equestrian trail. Have fun exploring!

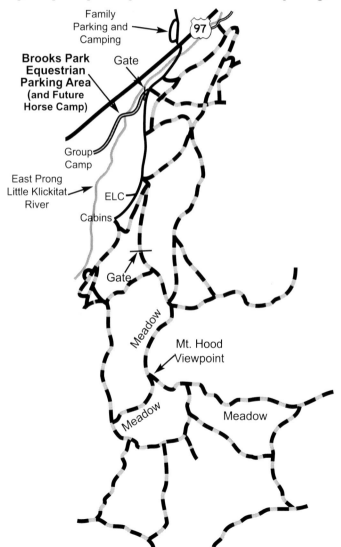

Queen Anne's lace

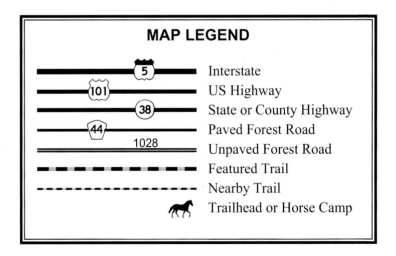

Capitol State Forest

Washington State Dept. of Natural Resources

Located just 5 miles south of Olympia, Capitol State Forest is a 100,000-acre working forest that is sustainably logged to help fund the public schools of Washington State. The forest is open for public recreation, with separate trails for motorized and non-motorized users. Non-motorized users can enjoy nearly 50 miles of trail from May 1 to November 30. The 4.5-mile Equine Loop (where bike riders are excluded) is open to horseback riders year round. The trails are a mix of mature second-growth forest and open clear-cuts that feature amazing displays of wildflowers in season. What a beautiful area!

Diana and Karen ride Scotty and Vaquero
across a flower-filled clear-cut area.

Getting to Capitol State Forest

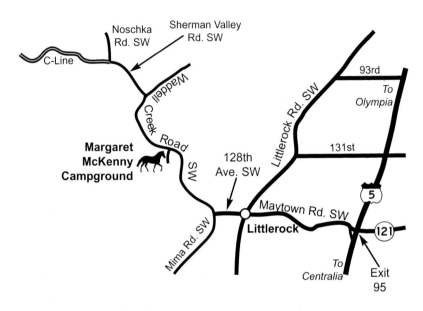

The trees at Margaret McKenny Campground dwarf the trailers.

Margaret McKenny Campground

Directions: From I-5 south of Olympia, take Exit 95 and head west on Maytown Road SW toward Littlerock. After 3 miles, the road goes through Littlerock and becomes 128th Ave. SW. Continue straight for another 0.8 mile and turn right on Waddell Creek Rd. SW. The campground is ahead on the left in 2.4 miles.

Elevation: 300 feet

Campsites: 24 sites, of which 6 allow horses. The horse sites are all back-in, with fire rings and picnic tables. Two sites have room for 2 trailers. Four sites have a 1-horse corral, 2 have double corrals (though strangely, they're not the same sites that can hold 2 trailers). All corrals have concrete floors. When we were there, some corrals were missing their chain gates. Each site has its own manure bin. All sites have room for highlining.

Facilities: Toilet. Stock water from a hand pump, though the water pump is a long way from some of the campsites. The day-use area has parking for 10 trailers, plus a toilet, manure bin, picnic table, and highline poles.

Permits: Discover Pass required for camping or day use

Season: May 1 to November 30

Contact: Washington State Dept. of Natural Resources, 360-825-1631

Capitol Forest Trails

Trail	Difficulty	Elevation	Round Trip
Equine Loop	Moderate	300-550	4 miles
Greenline/Wedekind Loop	Challenging	550-1,700	9.5 miles
Lost Valley Loop	Moderate	500-1,200	8 miles
McKenny/Mima Loop	Moderate	3,00-1,200	13 miles
Mima Falls Loop	Moderate	250-650	7.5 miles

Equine Loop

Trailhead: Start at Margaret McKenny Campground

Length: 4 miles round trip

Elevation: 300 to 550 feet

Difficulty: Moderate

Footing: Hoof protection suggested

Season: Year round

Permits: Discover Pass required for camping or day-use

Facilities: Toilet, stock water, highline poles, and manure bin at the day-use area. No stock water on the trail.

Highlights: This short loop provides a nice orientation to the trails near Margaret McKenny Campground. The Equine Loop segment of this trail is also the only non-motorized trail at Capitol State Forest that doesn't allow mountain bikes. The trail goes through some mature forest and some clear cuts, so even though it's a short ride there is variety in what you will see. There's even a view of Mt. Rainier!

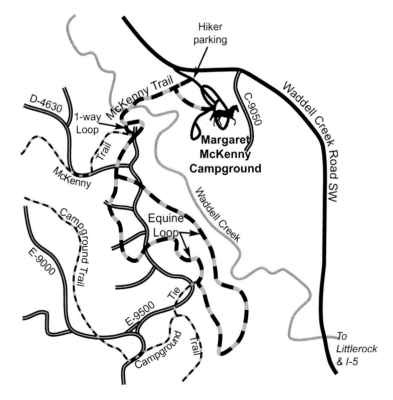

Donna on Zoey and Nancy on Sundance,
on the Equine Loop Trail.

The Ride: Pick up the McKenny Trail on the southwest end of the day-use area, across the road and a little west of the entrance to the horse camp loop. In 0.2 mile, you'll reach a junction and turn left. (Going right takes you the hiker parking area.) Ride 0.3 mile, crossing the bridge over Waddell Creek and going up the hill to a junction where a sign on the left fork of the trail says "Do Not Enter." Take the right fork and it will put you on a short one-way loop. In 0.1 mile, you'll reach a trail junction at a gravel road. The trail straight ahead is the other leg of the one-way loop, which you'll take to return to your trailer. The trail to your hard right is the continuation of the McKenny Trail. Instead, turn right on the gravel road and in 50 feet turn right again on the Equine Loop. Follow it for 0.2 mile to the 3-way junction where the loop part of the Equine Loop Trail begins. To ride the loop counter-clockwise, turn right. In 0.9 mile, the tie trail that connects to the Campground Trail goes to the right. Make a hard left to stay on the Equine Loop. Follow it for 1.3 miles back to the 3-way junction where the loop section began. Turn right and retrace your steps back to the parking area (but this time you'll go around the one-way loop to the right).

Greenline/Wedekind Loop

Trailhead: Start at Fall Creek Trailhead

Length: 9.5 miles round trip

Elevation: 550 to 1,700 feet

Difficulty: Challenging -- trail is very popular with mountain bikes, and has short lines of sight in many places

Footing: Hoof protection recommended

Season: May 1 to November 30

Permits: Discover Pass required for camping or day-use

Facilities: Toilet, highline poles, and manure bin at the Fall Creek day-use area. Stock water at nearby Fall Creek. No stock water on the trail.

Highlights: This trail is very popular with mountain bike riders, who love to careen down from near the summit of Capitol Peak. If you do this ride on a weekday when mountain bike traffic is light, it can be great fun. On a busy summer weekend, though, it could be a nightmare. The trail runs through Douglas-fir forest characterized by short

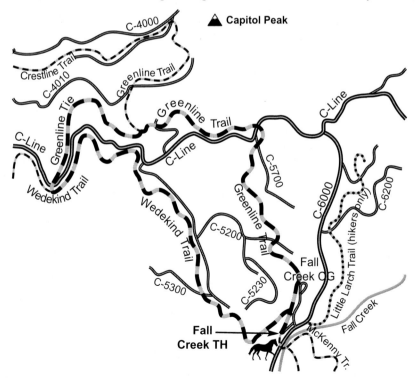

lines of sight and many blind corners, then it runs through clear-cut areas that offer better visibility. It's best to ride the loop counter-clock-wise, so you face the mountain bike riders head-on as they speed down off Capitol Peak on the Greenline Trail. The forested segments are beautiful, and the clear-cuts offer spectacular seasonal wildflowers and nice views of Mt. Rainier.

Getting to Fall Creek Trailhead: Follow the driving directions at the beginning of this chapter for Margaret McKenny Campground, but in-stead of turning into the campground, stay on Waddell Creek Road SW for an additional 1.7 miles, then turn left on Sherman Valley Rd. SW. Continue 1.4 miles, and at the intersection with Noschka Rd, go straight on the (gravel) C-Line Road. After 2.4 miles, turn left on C-6000 and follow it 1.8 miles to the trailhead. Four-wheel drive is rec-ommended.

The Ride: Pick up the Greenline Trail on the north end of the parking area. In 0.3 mile you'll pass the junction with the Wedekind Trail. Stay to the right and continue 3.4 miles to the junction where the Greenline Trail continues to the right toward Capitol Peak and the Greenline Tie goes to the left. Veer left on the Greenline Tie Trail. In 1.5 miles you'll reach the junction with the Wedekind Trail. Turn left on it and in 4.2 miles you'll come to the junction with the Greenline Trail. Go right and in 0.3 mile you'll be back at the trailhead.

Diana on Scotty, Karen on Vaquera, and Nancy on Sundance, heading across a clear-cut on the Wedekind Trail.

Lost Valley Loop

Trailhead: Start at Fall Creek Trailhead
Length: 8 miles round trip
Elevation: 500 to 1,200 feet
Difficulty: Moderate
Footing: Hoof protection recommended
Season: May 1 to November 30
Permits: Discover Pass required for camping or day-use
Facilities: Toilet, highline poles, and manure bin at the Fall Creek day-use area. Stock water at nearby Fall Creek. No stock water on the trail.

Highlights: This trail circles a ridge, following Sherman Creek along the western side of the loop. If you ride it clockwise, all of the elevation gain will come on the initial leg of the loop, followed by a more gradual descent to Sherman Creek, then a fairly level jaunt along the creek.

Getting to Fall Creek Trailhead: Follow the directions at the beginning of this chapter for Margaret McKenny Campground, but instead of turning into the campground, stay on Waddell Creek Road SW for

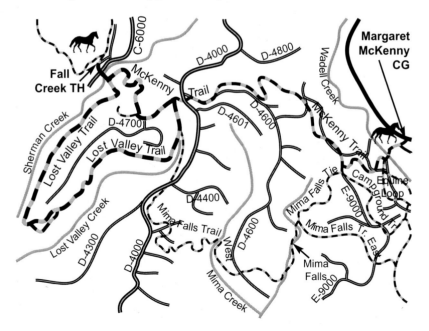

Karen rides Vaquera on the Lost Valley Trail.

an additional 1.7 miles, then turn left on Sherman Valley Rd. SW. Continue 1.4 miles, and at the intersection with Noschka Rd, go straight on the (gravel) C-Line Road. After 2.4 miles, turn left on C-6000 and follow it 1.8 miles to the trailhead. Four-wheel drive is recommended.

The Ride: From Fall Creek Trailhead, pick up the McKenny Trail on the south side of the parking area. In 0.4 mile the Lost Valley Trail comes in on the right. This will be your return route, so for now stay left to remain on the McKenny Trail. The trail climbs the side of a ridge and then begins to descend, reaching a second junction with the Lost Valley Trail after 2.1 miles. Turn right on the Lost Valley Trail, and in 0.4 mile the Mima Falls Trail West goes off on the left. Stay right and continue on the Lost Valley Trail for about 2.3 miles, steadily losing elevation. The trail then rounds the south end of the ridge and runs along Sherman Creek for 2.3 miles. When you reach the junction with the McKenny Trail, turn left on it to return to the trailhead.

Bonus Ride: You can also do this trail from Margaret McKenny Campground, for a 16.5-mile ride. Pick up the McKenny Trail on the southwest side of the McKenny day-use area and follow it 4.7 miles to the junction with the Lost Valley Trail, then turn left.

McKenny/Mima Loop

Trailhead: Start at the day-use area at Margaret McKenny Campground

Length: 13 miles round trip

Elevation: 300 to 1,200 feet

Difficulty: Moderate

Footing: Hoof protection recommended

Season: May 1 to November 30

Permits: Discover Pass required for camping or day-use

Facilities: Toilet, stock water, highline poles, and manure bin at the day-use area. Stock water is available on the trail.

Highlights: This delightful trail showcases the various life stages of a working forest as it runs through mature stands of Douglas-fir, through tree plantations, and through recent clear-cuts. From several vantage points you'll have views of Mt. Rainier. Wildflowers are abundant along the trail in early summer.

The Ride: Pick up the McKenny Trail on the southwest end of the day-use area, across the road and a little west of the entrance to the horse camp loop. Follow it 0.6 mile, over a bridge to a trail junction

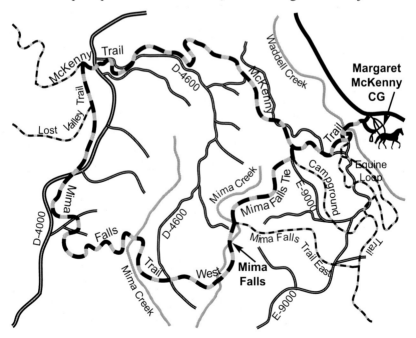

at a gravel road. (See the Equine Loop pages in this chapter for more details.) Make a hard right turn to stay on the McKenny Trail. In 0.8 mile, you'll reach the junction with the Campground Trail. Veer right to stay on the McKenny Trail. In 3.3 miles you'll reach an unsigned junction. Veer left, and in 200 yards you'll come to the junction of the McKenny Trail and the Lost Valley Trail. Turn left on the Lost Valley Trail and follow it for 0.4 mile, then veer left onto the Mima Falls Trail West. Continue on the Mima Falls Trail West for 5 miles. When you come to a picnic table and hitching rail in a clearing, you're at Mima Falls. Tie your horse and scramble down the foot trail to the left of the picnic table, which will take you to the base of the falls. After enjoying the view, continue on the Mima Falls Trail West for 0.3 mile to another unsigned junction. Go to the right and take the bridge over the creek. In 100 yards you'll come to a signed 3-way junction with the Mima Falls Trail East and the Mima Falls Tie Trail. Turn left on the Mima Falls Tie. In 1 mile you'll come to a 3-way junction with the Campground Trail. Turn left here and in 0.2 mile you'll reach the 3-way junction with the McKenny Trail. Turn right here and retrace your steps to the trailhead.

Diana on Scotty and Karen on Vaquera, in a flower-filled clear-cut on the Mima Falls Trail West.

Mima Falls Loop

Trailhead: Start at the day-use area at Margaret McKenny Campground

Length: 7.5 miles round trip

Elevation: 250 to 650 feet

Difficulty: Moderate

Footing: Hoof protection recommended

Season: May 1 to November 30

Permits: Discover Pass required for camping or day-use

Facilities: Toilet, stock water, highline poles, and manure bin at the day-use area. Stock water is available on the trail.

Highlights: If you'd like a shorter route to Mima Falls (pronounced MY-muh) than the McKenny/Mima Loop offers, this is the trail for you. It gains less elevation and it's quite a bit shorter. The forest is just as pretty as on the longer ride, and the waterfall is a delight.

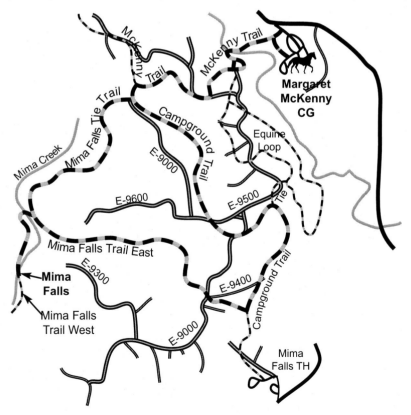

Mima Falls

The Ride: The McKenny Trail departs on the southwest end of the day-use area, across the road and a little west of the entrance to the horse camp loop. Follow it for 0.6 mile, over a bridge to a trail junction at a gravel road. (See the Equine Loop pages in this chapter for more details.) Make a hard right turn to stay on the McKenny Trail. In 0.8 mile you'll reach the junction with the Campground Trail. Turn left here, and in 0.2 mile the Mima Falls Tie Trail goes off to the right. This will be your return route. For now, veer left to stay on the Campground Trail and ride it 1.0 mile to the Tie Trail that connects to the Equine Loop. Stay to the right, and in another 0.9 mile turn right on the Mima Falls Trail East. In 1.5 miles it will take you to the 3-way junction with the Mima Falls Trail West and the Mima Tie Trail. Turn left on the Mima Falls Trail West and in 100 yards you'll come to an unsigned junction. Go to the left here, and in 0.3 mile you'll reach the picnic table and hitching rail at the falls. Tie your horse and scramble down the trail to the left of the picnic table to see the falls. Then retrace your steps back to the 3-way junction and turn left on the Mima Falls Tie Trail. In 1 mile you'll come to a junction with the Campground Trail. Turn left here and in 0.2 mile you'll reach the junction with the McKenny Trail. Turn right on it to return to the trailhead.

Tiger Lily

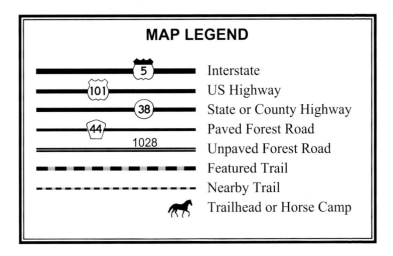

MAP LEGEND

5	Interstate
101	US Highway
38	State or County Highway
44	Paved Forest Road
1028	Unpaved Forest Road
	Featured Trail
	Nearby Trail
🐎	Trailhead or Horse Camp

Cody
Horse Camp

Gifford Pinchot National Forest

It's every horseman's dream: a Forest Service official who "gets" the whole idea of equestrian trail riding. Harry Cody, former district ranger in the Cowlitz Valley Ranger District, was that kind of Forest Service manager, and the very nice Cody Horse Camp is his legacy. The 26-mile Klickitat Trail, developed by volunteers from Back Country Horsemen, runs right past Cody Horse Camp. The horse camp lies in the valley carved by the Cispus River valley and is surrounded by steep ridges, so all of the riding here involves some elevation gain. If you head north on the Klickitat Trail you'll have a steep out-and-back ride to Elk Peak that offers panoramic views. If you head east on the Klickitat Trail the elevation changes aren't as significant and you can connect with other trails to create several loops of varying lengths. If your horse is in condition to handle the elevation changes of the surrounding terrain, you can easily fill a long weekend with nice rides at Cody Horse Camp.

*Linda rides Beamer on the Spring Creek Trail
near Cody Horse Camp.*

51

Getting to Cody Horse Camp

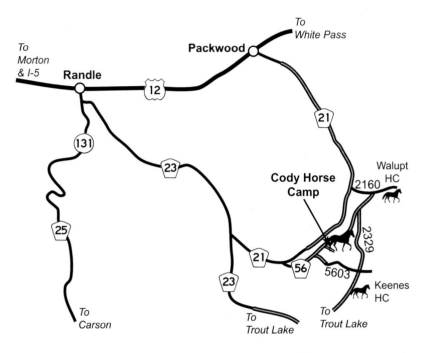

Most pull-throughs at Cody Horse Camp are long enough for 2 rigs.

Cody Horse Camp

Directions: From I-5, take Exit 68 (Yakima/White Pass) and head east on Hwy. 12. After 48.5 miles, in Randle, turn right on Hwy. 131. When the road makes a Y in 1 mile, veer left on Road 23. Follow it for 17.5 miles, then turn left on Forest Road 21 and continue 4.6 miles. Turn right on Road 56 and drive 4.9 miles, then turn right on Road 059 to reach the campground in 0.1 mile. **NOTE:** As of our publication date, Road 23 was closed due to a washout. Check with the Forest Service for access information before you make plans to visit.

Elevation: 3,100 feet

Campsites: 16 sites with highlines and cables. All sites are pull-throughs and most have room for 2 vehicles. All are gravel and fairly level. All sites have fire pits and picnic tables.

Facilities: Toilet, manure bins, potable water from a hand pump that also fills a stock water trough. When we were there the water wasn't working, but we found a good horse watering spot at the Muddy Fork just across the entrance road to the horse camp. The day-use area has an accessible mounting ramp and parking for 4-5 trailers.

Season: Summer through fall

Permits: None

Contact: Cowlitz Valley Ranger District, 360-497-1100

Cody Area Trails

Trail	Difficulty	Elevation	Round Trip
Elk Peak	Difficult	3,000-5,500	6-10 miles
Klickitat/PCT Loop	Challenging	3,000-5,200	17.5 miles
Midway Meadows Loop	Moderate	3,000-4,750	8.5 miles
Spring Creek Loop	Moderate	3,000-4,400	14 miles

Elk Peak

Trailhead: Start at Cody Horse Camp

Length: 6 miles round trip to a rock outcropping with views of the Goat Rocks and Mt. Adams, or 10 miles round trip to Elk Peak

Elevation: 3,000 to 4,150 feet to the rock overlook, or 3,000 to 5,500 feet to Elk Peak

Difficulty: Difficult -- steep trail. Horses should be in good condition.

Footing: Hoof protection recommended

Season: Summer through fall

Permits: None

Facilities: Toilet, potable water, stock trough, and manure bins at the horse camp. Day-use parking for 4-6 trailers. Stock water is available at the Cispus River crossing, but not after you begin climbing the ridge.

Highlights: The first 1.5 miles of this trail are easy and mostly level, but the crossing of the Cispus River is not suitable for green horses or

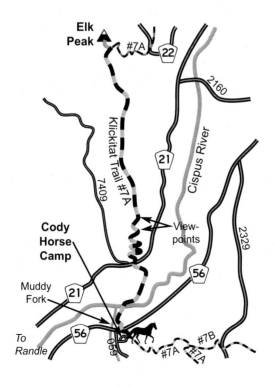

riders. After that, the trail is very steep. Even if your horse is in good condition, you'll need to stop and rest him frequently.

The Ride: Pick up the Klickitat Trail #7A across from campsite 7. When the trail forks in 50 feet, turn left. In 0.2 mile, the trail crosses Road 56, runs past a couple of primitive campsites, and begins following a decommissioned forest road. In 0.6 mile, you'll ford the Cispus River, which is very wide and shallow but the rocky, muddy banks of the river can be a bit challenging. You'll continue on a single-track trail and then a forest road that will take you to Road 21 in another mile. The trail crosses Road 21 and begins making switchbacks up a high ridge, gaining 1,000 feet in the next 1.3 miles. In places the trail has a 30% grade. From a couple of rock outcroppings along the trail in this section, you'll have views of the Goat Rocks and Mt. Adams. From there, the trail runs up the crest of the ridge for 2 miles, steadily gaining another 1,000 feet of elevation until it passes near the summit of Elk Peak. A very steep and rocky spur trail will take you the last 300 feet to the top of the peak. Tie your horse down below and hike the last stretch to the summit, where you can enjoy the panoramic view.

Linda and Beamer go past a viewpoint on the Klickitat Trail.

Klickitat/PCT Loop

Trailhead: Start at Cody Horse Camp

Length: 17.5 miles round trip

Elevation: 3,000 to 5,200 feet

Difficulty: Challenging -- long, with a couple of steep traverses on the Pacific Crest Trail

Footing: Hoof protection recommended

Season: Summer through fall

Permits: None

Facilities: Toilet, potable water, stock trough, and manure bins at the horse camp. Day-use parking for 4-6 trailers. Stock water is available on the trail.

Highlights: This is a rather long ride, but the mountain views and the beautiful terrain are well worth it. The Pacific Crest Trail has a few steep side slopes, but this ride is very do-able if your horse is in good condition.

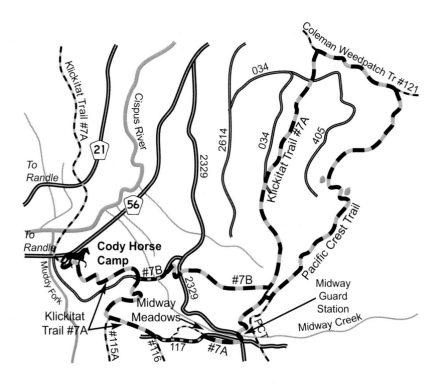

The Ride: Pick up the Klickitat Trail #7A across from campsite 7. When the trail forks in 50 feet, turn right. In 1.3 miles, Trail #7B comes in on a dirt road on the left. Go straight on the Klickitat Trail for another 1.1 miles, then veer left to stay on it at the junction with the Spring Creek Trail #115A. In 0.6 mile, stay left again at the junction with the High Lakes Trail #116 and follow the Klickitat Trail as it runs along dirt Road 117 for 0.6 mile to Midway Meadows. Then veer right off Road 117 on a single track trail that will take you to Road 2329 in 0.5 mile. Turn left and ride along Road 2329 to cross over Midway Creek, then continue on the Klickitat Trail as it departs from Road 2329 on the right. Follow the trail 0.9 mile more and turn right on a well-defined but unsigned tie trail to reach the PCT in 50 feet. Turn left on the PCT and follow it 4.1 miles to the Coleman Weedpatch Trail #121. Turn left, and in 1.2 miles you'll reach the junction with the Klickitat Trail #7A. Turn left and continue 3.5 miles to the junction with Trail #7B. Turn right at this junction and follow Trail #7B for 0.9 mile to Road 2329, cross it, and continue 0.5 mile to a dirt road. Follow Trail #7B to the left on the dirt road for 0.2 mile. When it intersects with the Klickitat Trail #7A, turn right on it and retrace your steps to return to the horse camp.

Linda and Beamer cruise along the Klickitat Trail #7A.

Midway Meadows Loop

Trailhead: Start at Cody Horse Camp

Length: 8.5 miles round trip

Elevation: 3,000 to 4,750 feet

Difficulty: Moderate

Footing: Hoof protection recommended

Season: Summer through fall

Permits: None

Facilities: Toilet, potable water, stock trough, and manure bins at the horse camp. Day-use parking for 4-6 trailers. Stock water is available on the trail.

Highlights: Midway Meadows is a nice spot for lunch for both you and your horse. You'll have gained enough elevation en route to the meadows that your horse will be relaxed and listening to you, but not so much that you're both tired and cranky. The meadows are beautiful, and the nearby guard station building is historic.

The Ride: Pick up the Klickitat Trail #7A across from campsite 7. When the trail forks in about 50 feet, turn right. The trail runs steadily uphill, gaining about 800 feet of elevation in 1.3 miles before reaching the junction of the Klickitat Trail and Trail #7B (which comes in on the left on a dirt road). Cross the dirt road and continue on Trail

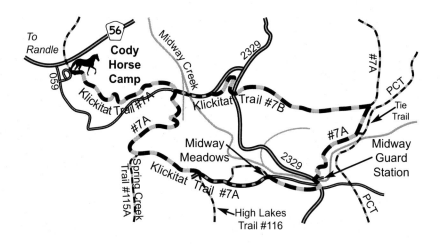

Jane grazes contentedly during a lunch break at Midway Meadows.

#7A for 1.1 mile. Just before you reach the junction of the Klickitat Trail and the Spring Creek Trail #115A, you'll traverse a steep hillside with a nice view of Mt. Adams and the Cispus River valley. At the Klickitat /Spring Creek Trail junction, veer left on the Klickitat Trail #7A and head uphill for 0.6 mile. When you reach the junction with the High Lakes Trail #116, veer left on a dirt road (Road 117) next to a sign saying "Midway Meadows." You'll reach Midway Meadows in 0.6 mile. From there, the Klickitat Trail veers off Road 117 to the right and parallels it for 0.5 mile to Road 2329. Turn left on Road 2329 to cross Midway Creek, then detour to the right to see the Midway Guard Station. You'll find a good place to water your horse behind the building. Return to Road 2329 and immediately pick up the Klickitat Trail on the right. Follow it for 0.9 mile to an unsigned tie trail on the right that leads to the PCT in 50 feet. Ignore it, stay to the left, and continue 0.3 mile to the junction with Trail #7B. Turn left on Trail #7B, and in 0.9 mile you'll cross gravel Road 2329. Continue another 0.5 mile to where the trail goes to the left and runs on a dirt road. Follow it 0.2 mile to the junction with the Klickitat Trail, then turn right and follow the Klickitat Trail 1.3 miles to return to your trailer.

Spring Creek Loop

Trailhead: Start at Cody Horse Camp

Length: 14 miles round trip

Elevation: 3,000 to 4,400 feet

Difficulty: Moderate

Footing: Hoof protection recommended

Season: Summer through fall

Permits: None

Facilities: Toilet, potable water, stock trough, and manure bins at the horse camp. Day-use parking for 4-6 trailers. Stock water is available on the trail.

Highlights: As you ride this fun trail, you'll pass through a variety of forest micro-environments, from dense groves of Douglas-firs (including some old growth), to open mixed-conifer forest with huckleberries, bear grass, and lupine in the understory, to arid lodgepole

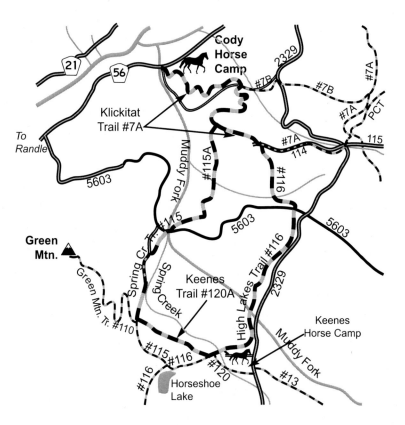

forest. You'll also pass several meadows that will invite your horse to stop and graze.

The Ride: Pick up the Klickitat Trail #7A across from campsite 7. When the trail forks in about 50 feet, turn right. The trail runs steadily uphill, gaining nearly 800 feet of elevation in 1.3 miles before reaching the junction of Trails #7A and #7B (which comes in on the left on a dirt road). Cross the dirt road and continue on Trail #7A for 1.1 mile to the junction with the Spring Creek Trail #115A. Turn right on the Spring Creek Trail #115A. It runs steeply downhill, then levels out as it runs through several different forest environments. In 1.9 miles you'll reach paved Road 5603. Turn right on the road and ride it across the Muddy Fork, then in 200 feet pick up the trail again on the left side of the road. In 0.4 mile the trail "T's" into a dirt road. Go left on the dirt road, and in 0.3 mile the road enters a dense wood and soon becomes a single-track trail. In another 0.7 mile, turn left on the Keenes Trail #120A. Follow it 1.1 miles to an unsigned junction with the High Lakes Trail #116. Turn left here. In another 0.2 mile the Keenes Trail #120 goes off to the right. Stay left, cross Spring Creek (a great place to water your horse), and ignore the unsigned trail that goes off to the right on the far side of the creek. Continue on the High Lakes Trail for 0.9 mile, cross the silty Muddy Fork, and in 1.6 miles you'll cross paved Road 5603 again. In another 1.1 miles, veer left on the Klickitat Trail #7A. In 0.6 mile you'll arrive at the junction of Trail #7A and Trail #115A. Veer right on Trail #7A and retrace your steps to the horse camp.

Linda and Beamer travel through a dense stand of Douglas-firs on the Spring Creek Trail #115A.

Birdsfoot trefoil

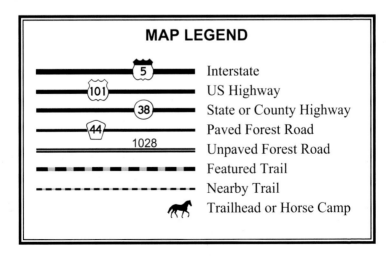

MAP LEGEND

Interstate

US Highway

State or County Highway

Paved Forest Road

Unpaved Forest Road

Featured Trail

Nearby Trail

Trailhead or Horse Camp

Day Rides, Columbia Gorge

Various National and State Agencies

At the end of the last Ice Age, an ice dam created Glacial Lake Missoula in present-day Montana. As the climate warmed, the ice dam gave way and released a torrent of floodwater that carved the Columbia Gorge and flooded much of eastern Washington and the Willamette Valley in Oregon. The ice dam froze over and then melted as many as 25 times, resulting in a series of catastrophic floods that created the spectacular landscape of today's Columbia Gorge. You can explore this landscape on horseback at the Catherine Creek area, at Columbia Hills State Park, and on the Klickitat Trail. Don't miss the spring wildflowers in the Gorge hills -- they're spectacular. And not far away, the Buck Creek Trail showcases the Cascade foothills terrain just north of the Gorge.

The Columbia River and the basalt cliffs of the Columbia Gorge, from Columbia Hills State Park.

Getting There

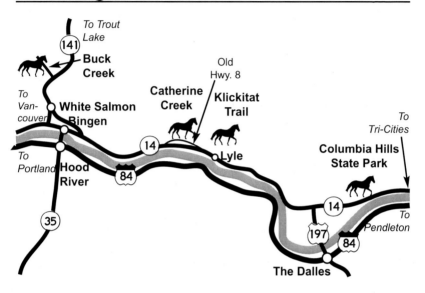

Columbia Gorge Trails

Trail	Difficulty	Elevation	Round Trip
Buck Creek Trail	Challenging	500-4,000	Up to 19 mi.
Catherine Creek	Moderate	250-1,500	Varies
Columbia Hills State Park	Moderate	350-1,300	7.5 miles
Klickitat Trail	Easy	100-450	Varies

Trails in the Columbia Gorge

Directions: See the pages in this chapter for each riding area

Elevation: 100-4,000 feet, depending on riding area chosen

Campsites: No overnight camping

Season: Varies by area

Contact: Buck Creek: Washington DNR, 360-577-2025
Catherine Creek: Columbia Gorge National Scenic Area, 541-308-1700
Columbia Hills State Park: Washington State Parks, 509-767-1159
Klickitat Trail: Columbia Gorge National Scenic Area, 541-308-1700

*Theresa and Breeze take a breather at Catherine Creek
on a hillside overlooking the Columbia Gorge.*

Buck Creek Trail

Trailhead: Start at the unnamed trailhead on Road B1000 or at Buck Creek Trailhead 1

Length: Up to 19 miles

Elevation: 500 to 4,000 feet

Difficulty: Challenging -- steep trail, large elevation changes, mountain bikes, limited lines of sight

Footing: Hoof protection recommended

Season: Summer through fall

Permits: Discover Pass required

Facilities: Trailhead 1 has a toilet, 4 corrals with no chain gates, picnic table, and parking for 3-4 trailers. The unnamed trailhead on Road B1000 has a toilet, picnic tables, and loop parking for 2-3 trailers (depending on where hikers are parked).   No stock water on the trail.

Highlights: Located between White Salmon and Trout Lake, DNR's Buck Creek Trail explores the hills around Nestor Peak, Penny Ridge, and Baldy Peak and connects to the Monte Cristo Trail #52 and Monte Carlo Trail #53 on the Gifford Pinchot National Forest. The trails are shared with mountain bike riders, who typically ride the loop counter-clockwise.

Getting to Unnamed Trailhead: From Hwy. 14 about 2.8 miles west of Bingen, turn north on Hwy. 141-Alt. Go 2.9 miles, and at the junction turn left on Hwy. 141. Continue 1.9 miles and turn left on Northwestern Lake Road (B1000).   In 0.4 mile the

The Buck Creek trails are well signed with white diamonds on the trees.

road turns to gravel. Stay on B1000 for another 3.1 miles. The trailhead is on the left.

Getting to Buck Creek Trailhead 1: Follow the directions above, but after 0.9 mile on Road B1000, turn left on Nestor Peak Road (N1000), a one-lane gravel road with occasional turnouts. In 1.8 miles, turn right on a dirt road at a sign pointing to Trailhead #1. The trailhead is at the end of the road in 0.2 mile. Four-wheel drive is recommended.

The Ride: The 19-mile Buck Creek Trail runs through beautiful woods as it explores the hills around Buck Creek. The trails are very steep in places, they gain and lose significant elevation, and some lines of sight are limited so you may not be able to see a bicyclist coming. Your horse will need to be well-conditioned and not easily spooked by mountain bikes. You can vary your ride by connecting segments of the Buck Creek Trail with the area's many forest roads.

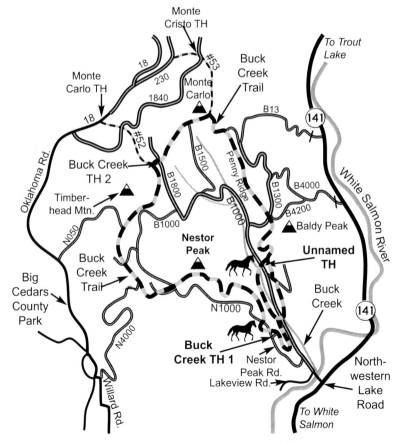

Catherine Creek

Trailhead: Start at the Catherine Creek Trailhead on the side of Old Hwy. 8. The trailheads in the Burdoin and Coyote Wall areas do not have trailer parking.

Length: Varies by route selected

Elevation: 250 to 1,500 feet

Difficulty: Moderate

Footing: Hoof protection a must

Season: Horses are permitted on the trails from May 1 to November 30. Note that horses are not permitted on trails Ca1, Ca2, Ca4, and on Co7 west of the Co7/Co8 junction.

Permits: None

Facilities: Parking for 5-6 trailers, depending on where hiker cars are parked. Stock water is available on the trail on a seasonal basis only -- no water by mid-summer.

Highlights: While some of the trails in the Catherine Creek/Coyote/Burdoin area are not horse friendly, if you stick with the ones designated for horses you'll have a splendid ride. Trail Ca3, the primary

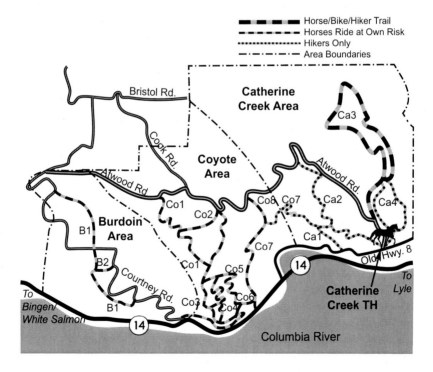

horse trail, travels beneath cliffs of columnar basalt (including a natural rock bridge), past an old homestead (the corrals are still standing but the cabin is a pile of rubble), through oak woodlands, and across open hillsides with expansive views of the Gorge, the Columbia River, and Mt. Hood. You can also ride all of Atwood Road. Trails Co1 through Co6, Co8, part of Co7, B1, and B2 are open to horses on a ride-at-your-own-risk basis. Beware: they feature plenty of bike traffic plus narrow, steep trails with steep side slopes, drop-offs, and cliffs. Trails Ca1, Ca2, Ca4, and part of Co7 are closed to horses.

Getting to Catherine Creek: From Bingen, drive east on Hwy. 14 for 4.5 miles and turn left on Old Hwy. 8. Follow it 1.4 miles and park in the gravel turnout on the north side of the road, across from the sign for Catherine Creek.

The Ride: From the trailhead, pick up the road signed as Road 020. In 0.3 mile you'll reach a junction. Atwood Road goes off to the left and Ca3 goes off to the right. Have fun exploring this beautiful area!

Theresa rides Breeze through oak woodlands and past
the remains of an old corral in the Catherine Creek Area.

Columbia Hills State Park

Trailhead: Start at the Crawford Oaks Trailhead or at the Dalles Mountain Ranch Upper Trailhead

Length: 7.5 miles round trip

Elevation: 350 to 1,300 feet

Difficulty: Moderate

Footing: Hoof protection recommended

Season: April through November

Permits: Discover Pass required

Facilities: Both trailheads have toilets and hitching rails. Crawford Oaks has parking for 6 trailers. The upper trailhead has a panoramic view and parking for 3-4 trailers. Stock water is available on the trail.

Highlights: The delightful Crawford Oaks/Dalles Mountain Ranch Trails explore the hills above the Columbia Gorge, providing panoramic views of the Columbia River, Mt. Hood, the basalt formations in the Gorge, and the nearby grass-covered hills. In spring the wildflowers are stunning. The trails run steadily up and down the hills, but they aren't overly steep and there aren't any dropoffs. The 3,338-

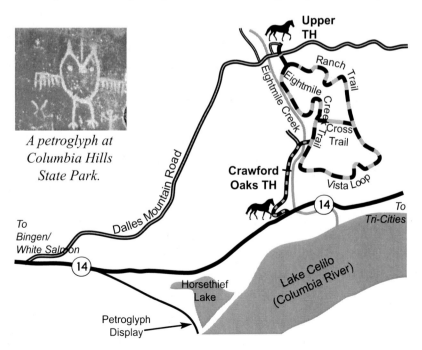

A petroglyph at Columbia Hills State Park.

Theresa and Breeze enjoy the panoramic views on the Vista Loop.

acre park's trails are open to horses, hikers, and mountain bikes. On your way to or from the ride, be sure to stop and check out the park's fascinating display of petroglyphs that were preserved just before The Dalles Dam flooded the lower elevations of the Gorge.

Getting There: From Bingen, drive east on Hwy. 14 for 22 miles. Just past milepost 87, turn left into the Crawford Oaks trailhead. If you want to go to the upper trailhead instead, turn left on Dalles Mountain Road between mileposts 84 and 85 and follow the gravel road for 3.7 miles. As you approach the ranch buildings, turn left on the second dirt road and follow it 0.1 mile to the upper trailhead.

The Ride: From the Crawford Oaks trailhead, the trail follows a gravel road up over a basalt cliff and then along Eightmile Creek, which is lined with tall oak and maple trees. In 0.5 mile, you'll go through a gate, then 0.3 mile later you'll veer right on a signed dirt road. The trail follows the dirt road for 0.3 mile to a junction. Turn right on the Vista Loop, which provides spectacular views as it runs across the hills. After 1.9 miles, at the junction with the Cross Trail, veer right on the Ranch Trail. Follow it for 1.5 miles, then at the junction with the Eightmile Creek Trail, turn right and continue 0.2 mile to the Upper Trailhead. After taking in the view, return to the last junction and turn right on the Eightmile Creek Trail. It follows the creek and one of its tributaries for 1.2 miles to the junction with the Cross Trail. Stay to the right here, and in 0.2 mile you'll arrive at the junction with the Vista Loop. Turn right to return to the trailhead.

Klickitat Trail

Trailhead: Start at the Lyle Trail Access or the Klickitat Trail Access.

Length: 13 miles one way

Elevation: 100 feet at Lyle to 450 feet at Klickitat

Difficulty: Easy

Footing: Hoof protection a must

Season: Klickitat segment is open year round; Swale Canyon segment is closed to horses

Permits: None

Facilities: Parking for 3 trailers at the Lyle Trail Access, plus a toilet and seasonal drinking fountain. The Klickitat Trail Access has parking for a 2-3 trailers, depending on where hiker cars are parked. No stock water on the trail.

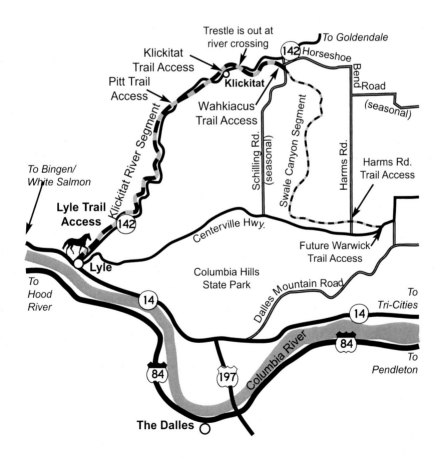

Highlights: The Klickitat Trail is a 31-mile rails-to-trails conversion, 13 miles of which is open to horses. (The Swale Canyon segment is not horse friendly, with many trestles and very rocky footing in places.) The Klickitat segment, which is open to horses, parallels the nationally-designated Wild and Scenic Klickitat River as it runs from Lyle to the town of Klickitat. The first 1.6 miles is paved, and after that the footing is crushed gravel. The trail offers excellent views of the river and the surrounding hills, and the spring wildflowers are stunning. Fall is also a great time to ride here because in October members of the Yakama Nation can be seen dip-netting for salmon from platforms built precariously along the cliffs above the river.

Getting To the Lyle Trail Access: Travel east on Hwy. 14 from Bingen/White Salmon for 9.3 miles. Immediately after crossing the Klickitat River in Lyle, turn left on Hwy. 142 toward Klickitat. In 400 feet, turn left into the trailhead parking area.

Getting to the Klickitat Trail Access: Follow the directions above, but stay on Hwy. 142 for 13.2 miles. Drive through the town of Klickitat and turn left into an old rail yard with an information kiosk for the Klickitat Trail.

The Ride: The trail departs from the north end of the parking area in Lyle. It runs beside the river, which flows through a deep and increasingly narrow chasm for the first 2 miles. Then the trail crosses the river on a concrete bridge, and soon afterward the river widens out and the trail runs along its bank. Ride as far as you like, then retrace your steps to return to the trailhead. Or you can do a trailer shuttle and leave one rig at the Klickitat Trail Access, then drive to the Lyle Trail Access and ride the Klickitat segment of the trail one way.

Theresa and Breeze amble along the Klickitat Trail.

The"Water Spirit" petroglyph at Columbia Hills State Park

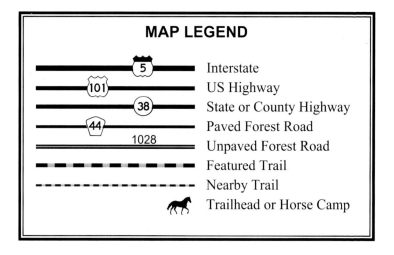

MAP LEGEND

5	Interstate
101	US Highway
38	State or County Highway
44	Paved Forest Road
1028	Unpaved Forest Road
	Featured Trail
	Nearby Trail
🐎	Trailhead or Horse Camp

Day Rides, Vancouver

Vancouver Parks & Recreation and Others

Everybody wants places to ride that are close to home and that offer year-round riding opportunities. Vancouver Parks and Recreation offers several equestrian riding areas that meet these criteria for riders who live in the southern part of Clark County. Whipple Creek Park in Ridgefield, Moulton Falls Park near Battle Ground, and the Washougal Dike at Capt. William Clark Park on the Columbia River all offer year-round trails that are open to horses. With these trails available, you don't have any excuse for not riding in the winter. Two other areas, Siouxon Creek and Saddle Dam, are relatively close to town but are at higher elevations so these trails can add some variety to your close-in riding in summer and fall when the trails are dry.

Lisa rides Jane on the Moulton Falls Trail.

Getting There

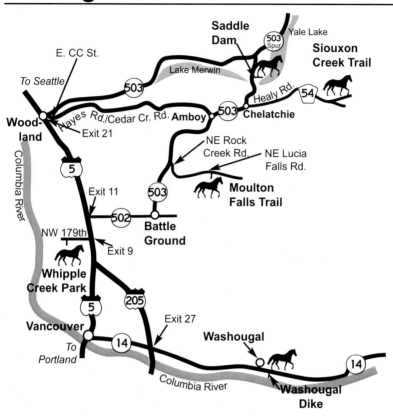

Vancouver Area Trails

Trail	Difficulty	Elevation	Round Trip
Moulton Falls Trail	Easy	550-700	5 miles
Saddle Dam	Moderate	500-1,100	4-5 miles
Siouxon Creek Trail	Moderate	1,150-1,850	10.5-14.5 mi.
Washougal Dike	Easy	20-35	6 miles
Whipple Creek Park	Easy	100-200	5+ miles

Vancouver Area Day Rides

Directions: See pages in this chapter for each trail

Elevation: 20-1,100 feet, depending on riding area chosen

Campsites: No overnight camping

Season: Year round, though some trails can be slippery when wet

Contact: Moulton Falls Park: Vancouver Parks and Recreation, 360-487-8311

Saddle Dam Area: Pacificorp, http://www.pacificorp.com/about/or/washington/sd.html

Siouxon Creek Trail: Mt. St. Helens NVM, Gifford Pinchot National Forest, 360-449-7800

Washougal Dike Trail: Vancouver Parks and Recreation, 360-487-8311

Whipple Creek Park: Vancouver Parks and Recreation, 360-487-8311

Anita on Dream, Candace on Beau, Arthur on Indy, and Cheri on Monet, at Yale Lake in the Saddle Dam area.

Moulton Falls Trail

Trailhead:	Start at the Hantwick Road trailhead off NE Lucia Falls Road near Yacolt
Length:	5 miles round trip
Elevation:	550 to 700 feet
Difficulty:	Easy, though there are several bridges
Footing:	Hoof protection recommended
Season:	Year round
Permits:	None
Facilities:	Porta-potties, and pull-through parking for up to 6 trailers. No stock water on the trail.

Highlights: This trail follows an old roadbed from the Hantwick Road trailhead to Moulton Falls, paralleling the East Fork Lewis River as it tumbles over boulders and flows through deep green pools. The trail is wide and has little elevation gain. For the first 0.8 mile the trail is paved, and after that the footing is compacted gravel. Several tiny waterfalls cascade down the uphill side of the trail as tributary creeks flow to the river. Aside from the initial paved stretch, the trail has great footing for winter riding. In summer its dense shade provides a cool respite from the heat of the day.

Getting To the Hantwick Road Trailhead: From I-5, take Exit 11 and go east on Hwy. 502/NE 219th St. In 6 miles turn left on Hwy.

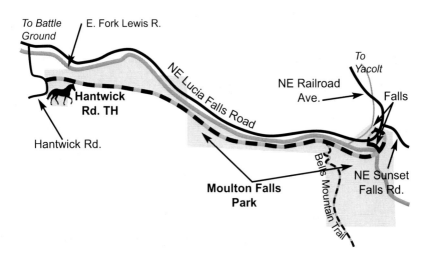

503/NE Lewisville Hwy. (NW 10th St.) Follow it 5.6 miles and turn right on NE Rock Creek Rd. In 0.3 mile the road becomes NE 152nd Ave. After 1.2 miles the road veers left and becomes NE Lucia Falls Road. About 5.3 miles after turning off Hwy. 503, turn right on Hantwick Road. In 0.4 mile, Hantwick Road makes a very sharp right turn and crosses a railroad track. The trailhead is on the left in 0.1 mile.

The Ride: Pick up the trail on the north side of the parking area. The first 0.8 mile of the trail is paved. After that, the tread is compacted gravel all the way to Moulton Falls. The trail crosses several bridges and culverts that span the tributary creeks tumbling down into the East Fork Lewis River. In 2.2 miles, you'll reach a junction with the Bells Mountain Trail. Stay to the left and in another 0.8 mile you'll reach the Moulton Falls area. At the falls parking area, there is a short loop trail that visits Moulton Falls and Big Tree Falls. Either way you go, though, you'll eventually reach flights of stairs, so horses cannot complete the loop trail at the falls. When you reach the falls parking area, turn around and retrace your steps to your trailer.

Lisa and Jane enjoy the Moulton Falls Trail
on a sunny spring day.

Saddle Dam Area

Trailhead: Start at the Saddle Dam Trailhead, off Hwy. 503

Length: 4.5 miles round trip on the Saddle Dam Trail, 4 miles round trip to Ghost Lake, 5 miles round trip to a viewpoint on a high shoulder of the mountain

Elevation: 500 feet at the trailhead to 750 feet on the Saddle Dam Trail, 850 feet at Ghost Lake, or 1,100 feet to the viewpoint

Difficulty: Mostly moderate, but there are some steep spots on all of the trails that can be slippery when wet, and the Saddle Dam trail has some steep side hills.

Footing: Hoof protection recommended

Season: Late spring through fall -- trails can be slippery when wet

Permits: None

Facilities: Toilet and pull-through parking for 8 trailers at the trailhead. Stock water is available on the trail.

Highlights: The trails and logging roads in the Saddle Dam area explore a mountainside northwest of the Saddle Dam at Yale Lake. You can ride to Frasier Pond or to a viewpoint on a high shoulder of the

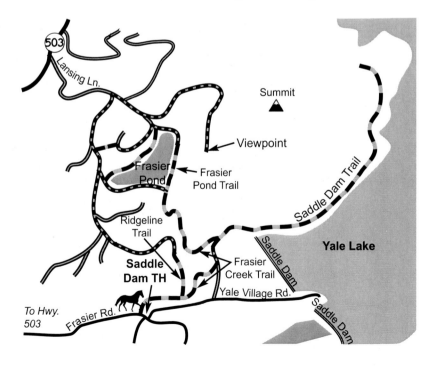

mountain (from which you can see Lake Merwin's Cresap Bay and Frasier Pond below you). You can take the Saddle Dam Trail, which roughly follows the shore of Yale Lake. Or you can just explore the logging roads in the area. An elk herd lives on this mountain. So do coyotes, so keep an eye on your dog.

Getting To the Saddle Dam Trailhead: From I-5 northbound, take the Woodland exit (Exit 21) and turn west on Hwy. 503/Lewis River Hwy. Immediately turn right on E. CC St. Cross the Lewis River and bear left, which will put you on NW Hayes Rd. Follow it for 5.3 miles and the road name changes to NE Cedar Creek Rd. Continue on NE Cedar Creek Road to Amboy, then go straight on Hwy. 503 toward Chelatchie. Continue on Hwy. 503 past the Chelatchie Prairie General Store for 3 miles and cross the one-lane bridge. Continue another 0.5 mile and turn right on Frasier Road. The trailhead is ahead on the left in 1 mile.

The Ride: The trail departs on the northwest side of the parking area. In 0.3 mile the Saddle Dam Trail goes straight ahead, and the trail to Ghost Lake and the viewpoint goes to the left. Some of the trail is single track and some is on logging roads. Some junctions are signed but most are not, so exploration is part of the fun of riding here.

From the viewpoint you can see Frasier Pond and Cresap Bay.

Siouxon Creek Trail

Trailhead: Start at the Lower Siouxon Trailhead
Length: 10.5 miles round trip to Siouxon Falls; 14.5 miles round trip to Chinook Falls
Elevation: 1,150 to 1,850 feet
Difficulty: Moderate: bridges, hikers, mountain bikes, and creek crossings with very slick rocks
Footing: Hoof protection suggested
Season: Summer through fall
Permits: None
Facilities: Parking for 2-3 trailers. No facilities. Stock water is available on the trail.

Highlights: Siouxon Creek (pronounced SOO-sahn, rhymes with Tucson) flows through a deep canyon between steep ridges. Huge Douglas-firs and cedars create dense shade, and oxalis, sword ferns, and a thick carpet of moss grow in the understory. Tributary streams cross the trail, often with small waterfalls on their uphill side. Siouxon Falls cascades 28 feet through a rock cleft into a deep green pool. Beautiful!

Getting to Lower Siouxon Trailhead: From I-5 northbound, take the Woodland exit (Exit 21) and turn west on Hwy. 503/Lewis River Hwy. Immediately turn right on E. CC St. Cross the Lewis River and bear

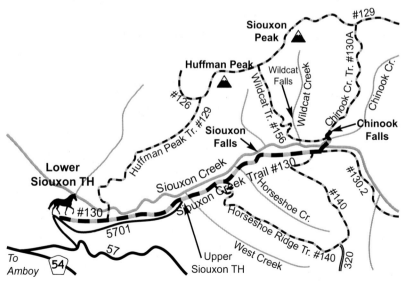

left, which will put you on NW Hayes Rd. Follow it for 5.3 miles and the road name changes to NE Cedar Creek Rd. Continue on NE Cedar Creek Road to Amboy and then go straight on Hwy. 503.   In Chelatchie, turn right on Healy Road (Road 54) next to the Chelatchie Prairie General Store. Watch your odometer closely, because from here on there are no road signs. In 9.1 miles you'll come to a fork where both roads are paved. Take the left fork, Road 57, which runs uphill. Continue 1.2 miles on pavement that is in poor condition, then veer left on paved but unsigned Road 5701. Follow it (again, the road is in poor shape) for 0.7 mile. At a hairpin turn, you'll find trailer parking at a turnout on the left side of the road. Don't continue to the Upper Siouxon Trailhead, as it has no room to turn your trailer around.

The Ride: Pick up the Siouxon Creek Trail #130 on the north side of Road 5701, about 100 yards along the road from the trailer parking turnout. In 1.4 miles from the trailer parking area, the Huffman Peak Trail #129 goes off to the left. Two miles later you'll reach the Upper Siouxon hiker trailhead. In 0.8 mile a connector trail to the Horseshoe Ridge Trail #140 goes off to the right, and 0.3 miles later the Horseshoe Ridge Trail itself goes off to the right. About 0.9 mile later, you'll come to a viewpoint overlooking the impressive Siouxon Falls. If you

continue up the Siouxon Creek Trail for another 2 miles you'll reach the junction with the Chinook Creek Trail #130A. Follow it about 0.3 mile to see beautiful Chinook Falls, which drops 68 feet off a rock cliff.

If you are tempted to ride the Huffman Peak, Wildcat, Chinook, and Horseshoe Ridge Trails, note that the first 3 of these trails involve deep and very challenging creek crossings, and the latter isn't recommended for horses because of its steep dropoffs.

Siouxon Falls

Washougal Dike

Trailhead:	Start at the west end of S. Index St. in Washougal
Length:	6 miles round trip
Elevation:	20 to 35 feet
Difficulty:	Easy
Footing:	Hoof protection suggested
Season:	Year round
Permits:	None
Facilities:	Parking for 3-4 horse trailers. Toilet at the car parking area on S. Index St. No stock water on the trail.

Highlights: In April 1806, Lewis and Clark camped near Cottonwood Creek for 6 days. To commemorate this event, in 2005 the site became Capt. William Clark Park. The park features an all-weather trail along the Washougal Dike (officially named the Cottonwood Beach Trail), which parallels the Columbia River eastward to the Steigerwald Wildlife Refuge. The trail is a wide, straight gravel road along the dike, so it is elevated above the surrounding terrain. It provides excellent footing even after heavy rains. For the first 1.7 miles, you'll have a forest of cottonwoods on your right and an industrial area and working factories on your left. After that, the trail runs beside the serene Steigerwald Wildlife Refuge on the left (sorry, horses must stay

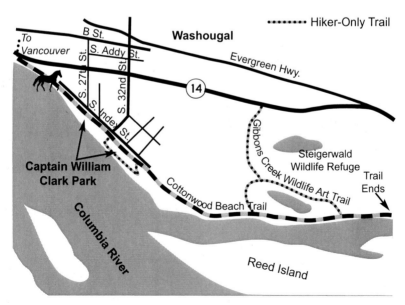

on the dike trail) and the Columbia River on the right. On a clear day you'll have a nice view of Mt. Hood.

Getting There: From I-205, take Exit 27 and head east on Hwy. 14. At milepost 17, turn right on S. 32nd St. In 0.5 mile, turn right on S. Index St. Continue 0.2 mile, then veer left at the junction with S. 27th St. to stay on S. Index St. Horse trailer parking is at the west end of S. Index St. Note that if you want to go west on Hwy. 14 to return home, you'll need to follow S. 27th St. north to S. Addy St. and turn right, then turn right again on S. 32nd St. and right again on Hwy. 14.

The Ride: Pick up the trail on the west end of S Index St. Your horse will have to step into and then out of a log box designed to prevent motor vehicles from accessing the trail. When you reach the top of the dike, turn left and follow it 3 miles to where the trail ends, then retrace your steps to return to your trailer.

The first part of the trail runs beside an industrial area.

After that, you'll have views of the Columbia River and Steigerwald Wildlife Refuge. On a clear day you can see Mt. Hood.

Whipple Creek Park

Trailhead: Start at the day-use parking area off NW 21st Ave. in Ridgefield

Length: Over 5 miles of trails

Elevation: 100 to 200 feet

Difficulty: Easy

Footing: Hoof protection suggested (gravel trails)

Season: Year round, but the trails may be muddy after rain

Permits: None

Facilities: Manure bin and parking for 10 trailers. No stock water on the trail.

Highlights: The Vancouver-Clark Parks and Recreation District describes Whipple Creek Park as an "undeveloped regional park." True enough, it has no ball diamonds and no manicured lawns. Instead, it features a nice network of trails through dense woods of mature Douglas-fir, maple and cedar. The trails, which are open to horses, hikers,

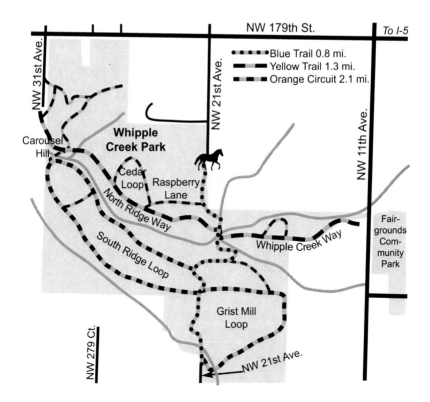

Lydia on Magic and Theresa on Breeze,
riding across a meadow at Whipple Creek Park.

and bikes, form several interconnected loops. The trail signs are color-coded as shown on the map legend at left, so it's tough to get lost here. In addition to the official trails, there are a number of user-created trails that offer supplemental riding options. In the future, a planned trail will run from Whipple Creek through the Fairgrounds Community Park to the Clark County Expo Center.

Getting To Whipple Creek Park: From I-5, take Exit 9 and head west on NW 179th St. In 1.5 miles, turn left on NW 21st Ave. Parking is at the end of the road in 0.4 mile.

The Ride: From the parking area at the end of NW 21st Ave., pick up the trail that heads south past the kiosk. From here, you can create your own loops of whatever length you like. While the trails are open year round, they can be very muddy during the wet season so volunteers have been working hard to gravel the trails where needed to create a more sustainable year-round trail tread. Note that the trail segments leading down to the creek that runs between North Ridge Way and South Ridge Loop are very steep and may be slippery when the trails are wet.

Scouler's hawkweed

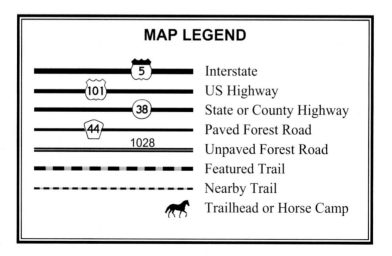

Falls Creek Horse Camp

Indian Heaven Wilderness, Gifford Pinchot NF

With its abundance of berries, fish, deer, elk, and camas, the Indian Heaven Wilderness has been a gathering place for Native American tribes for hundreds of years. You can explore the south end of the Wilderness from Falls Creek Horse Camp, which provides access to some exceptional trails both inside and outside of the Wilderness. You can ride to the historic Indian Race Track meadows, enjoy the panoramic views from the Red Mountain fire lookout, visit meadows of huckleberries and heather, ride past dozens of lakes, and check out a vast wet prairie. In late August when the huckleberries are ripe you can feast on this delicacy as you ride along. Heaven, indeed!

Teresa rides Pops and Lydia rides Magic on the Falls Creek Trail.

Getting to Falls Creek

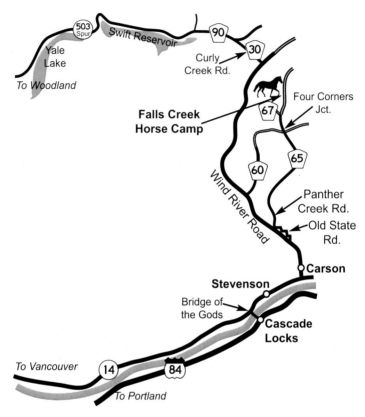

Pops in his portable corral and Tex on her highline at Falls Creek Horse Camp.

Falls Creek Horse Camp

Directions: From Stevenson, take Hwy. 14 east for 3.2 miles. Between mileposts 47 and 48, turn left on Wind River Hwy. toward Carson. In 5.8 miles, turn right on Old State Road, and almost immediately turn left on Panther Creek Road, which becomes Forest Road 65 in 0.9 mile. At milepost 10 you'll reach the Four Corners junction with Road 60. Go straight, and at milepost 12 the pavement ends and Road 67 goes to the left. Stay right and at milepost 15 you'll reach the horse camp on the left.

Elevation: 3,500 feet

Campsites: 4 sites with highline posts and cables, fire pits, and picnic tables. There are 2 pull-in sites, 2 back-in sites, and 2 overflow parking spaces. The campground road has a tight turning radius that is not suitable for larger rigs. (A 3-horse trailer without living quarters will have a very tight squeeze.) Note: you can park longer trailers in campsites 1 and 2, and then fairly easily back out of the campground to leave.

Facilities: Vault toilet. Stock water is available from Falls Creek, but it is a long way to carry water to some of the campsites.

Permits: None

Season: Summer through fall

Contact: Mt. Adams Ranger District, 509-395-3400

Falls Creek Area Trails

Trail	Difficulty	Elevation	Round Trip
Falls Creek Trail	Moderate	3,500-1,350	<18.5 mi.
Indian Race Track/Lakes Lp.	Moderate	3,500-5,000	14.5 miles
Indian Race Track/Red Mtn.	Moderate	3,500-4,900	6 miles
McClellan Meadows Loop	Moderate	3,000-4,000	10 miles

Falls Creek Trail

Trailhead: Start at Falls Creek Horse Camp

Length: 6 miles round trip to the Lava Cave Trailhead and the first lava cave, 14.5 miles round trip to the waterfall overlook, and 18.5 miles round trip to the end of the trail

Elevation: 3,500 to as low as 1,350 feet. Most of the elevation loss occurs in the last 2 miles of the trail.

Difficulty: Moderate

Footing: Hoof protection suggested

Season: Summer through fall, though mosquitoes can be fierce until mid-August

Permits: None

Facilities: Toilet, stock water from Falls Creek at the horse camp. No stock water on the trail.

Highlights: Falls Creek Trail roughly parallels its namesake creek but is rarely within sight or hearing of it. Instead, the beautiful forest is the primary focus of this trail unless you choose to ride all the way

to Falls Creek Falls. You'll find lava caves about 2.7 and 3.5 miles into the ride. The overlook for Falls Creek Falls is at mile 7.3. However, you can't see much of the waterfall from there. About 0.9 mile after the falls overlook you'll come to a junction with a side trail that runs steeply down to intersect with the hiker trail 0.2 mile below, and then continues to the left for 0.3 mile to the base of 200-foot Falls Creek Falls. We have not taken this spur trail but we understand that it is steep, crumbly, narrow, and exposed -- in other words, not safe for horses. Note that the Falls Creek Trail is a popular downhill mountain biking trail, so keep your ears open for approaching cyclists if you don't have a long line of sight along the trail.

The Ride: Falls Creek Trail #152 trail departs next to the first campsite on the left as you enter the campground. It runs gently but steadily downhill, roughly following the course of Falls Creek but almost never within sight of it. After 2.5 miles, the trail begins running along a dirt road, following it 0.3 mile to the Lava Caves trailhead on Road 6701, passing an interesting lava cave on the left on the way. There's a second lava cave on the right in another 0.8 mile, just before you reach Road 67. After Road 67, the trail continues down a gravel road that soon becomes a single-track trail again. After another couple of miles the trail veers close to the creek, then away again as the terrain begins to quickly lose elevation. In its first 7 miles the trail loses a little more than 1,000 feet. In the last 2.5 miles it loses another 1,000 feet before ending at Road 3062.

Teresa on Pops and Lydia on Magic, on the Falls Creek Trail.

Indian Race Track & Lakes Loop

Trailhead: Start at Falls Creek Horse Camp

Length: 14.5 miles round trip

Elevation: 3,500 to 5,000 feet

Difficulty: Moderate

Footing: Hoof protection a must

Season: Summer through fall, though mosquitoes can be fierce until mid-August

Permits: None

Facilities: Vault toilet, stock water at the horse camp. Stock water is available on the trail.

Highlights: This ride pretty much has it all: beautiful forest, meadows, hill climbs, panoramic vistas, and plenty of lakes. It follows the same route initially as the Indian Race Track/Red Mountain trail described in this chapter, but at the Indian Race Track it turns off and heads to the PCT, then goes on to Blue Lake and Thomas Lake before returning to the horse camp via Road 65. You'll have views of Mt. Hood and Mt. Adams as you travel over the flank of Berry Mountain,

and the lakes and meadows you'll encounter between Blue Lake and Thomas Lake are delightful.

The Ride: From the entrance to the horse camp, follow Road 65 to the left for 0.1 mile and turn right on the Indian Race Track Trail #171. Follow the trail across Falls Creek and up over a very rocky ridge. In 2.5 miles you'll reach the Race Track Lakes and the Indian Race Track meadows. In the meadows, turn left at the sign for Trail #171A (the sign simply points the way toward the Pacific Crest Trail), and in 0.6 mile you'll reach the PCT. Turn left, and soon the PCT begins climbing Berry Mountain. In the next 2 miles the trail gains 800 feet of elevation, providing views of Mt. Hood and Mt. Adams along the way. In this stretch, the trail traverses several steep side slopes, but the trail is wide and the steep spots are mercifully short. Then it descends 400 feet in 1.5 miles to arrive at beautiful Blue Lake, the most-visited lake in the Indian Heaven Wilderness. You'll find two good horse-watering spots along the lake shore. Here you'll leave the PCT, veering left on the Thomas Lake Trail #111. It takes you past a remarkable series of small lakes and meadows (mosquito nurseries in early and midsummer but usually dry by mid-August), passing between Thomas Lake on the left and Dee and Heather Lakes on the right before reaching Road 65 and the hiker trailhead. From here, turn left on gravel Road 65 and follow it 3.5 miles back to the horse camp.

Lydia on Magic and Teresa on Pops,
traveling along the shore of Blue Lake.

Indian Race Track/Red Mountain

Trailhead: Start at Falls Creek Horse Camp

Length: 6 miles round trip

Elevation: 3,500 to 4,900 feet

Difficulty: Moderate

Footing: Hoof protection a must

Season: Summer through fall, though mosquitoes can be fierce until mid-August

Permits: None

Facilities: Toilet, stock water from Falls Creek at the horse camp. Stock water is available on the trail.

Highlights: The area we now know as the Indian Heaven Wilderness has been a seasonal gathering place for local Indian tribes for centuries. They picked huckleberries, fished in the lakes, hunted deer and elk, and gathered roots. For fun, the young men raced their horses in the meadows. While you can no longer see evidence of the historic race track for which the meadows are named, it's easy to imagine the

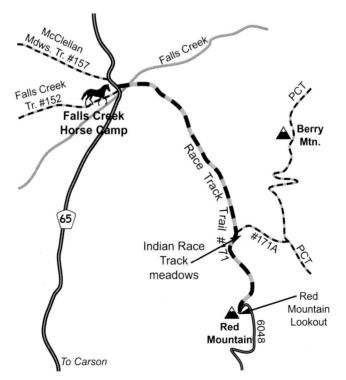

Teresa and Lydia give Pops and Magic a chance
to graze at the Indian Race Track meadows.

excitement of the events. From the Indian Race Track meadows, you can ride to the lookout at Red Mountain, the first fire lookout in Washington. From the summit you'll enjoy panoramic views of Mt. Hood, Mt. Adams, and Mt. St. Helens, plus the Big Lava Bed to the southeast and The Wart cinder cone to the south.

The Ride: From the entrance to the horse camp, turn left on Road 65. In 0.1 mile, pick up the Indian Race Track Trail #171 on the right. In 0.2 mile, you'll reach the Indian Heaven Wilderness sign. Shortly after that, a user trail goes off to the left. Ignore it and stay to the right, then ford Falls Creek next to the hiker bridge. The trail heads steadily up a ridge, and for the next 1.2 miles it is badly eroded and extremely rocky. After that the trail levels off a bit, and in another mile you'll reach the shallow Race Track Lakes and the famous meadows. At a sign pointing left toward the PCT, veer right. Then in 200 feet veer left at the wooden sign on the edge of the meadow to stay on Trail #171 as it heads toward the Red Mountain lookout. The trail can be somewhat indistinct in this section, but it soon reaches the trees and becomes easier to follow. The trail gains 500 feet in 0.8 mile as it climbs Red Mountain. From the lookout at the summit, enjoy the panoramic views, then retrace your steps to return to Falls Creek Horse Camp.

McClellan Meadows Loop

Trailhead: Start at Falls Creek Horse Camp

Length: 10 miles round trip

Elevation: 3,000 to 4,000 feet

Difficulty: Moderate

Footing: Hoof protection recommended

Season: Summer through fall, though mosquitoes can be fierce until mid-August

Permits: None

Facilities: Toilet, stock water from Falls Creek at the horse camp. No stock water on the trail.

Highlights: This pretty forested loop runs on nice trails that are part of the Oldman Pass ski trail network. The McClellan Meadows trail takes you steadily downhill to its namesake meadows, then the Terminator Trail takes you back up to Road 65, which you'll follow to return to the horse camp. There are no scenic vistas (other than a quick view of Mt. St. Helens from Road 65), but the forest is beautiful and

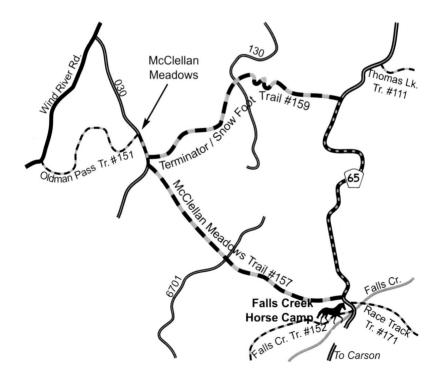

quite varied. McClellan Meadows is too wet to ride out into, but its huge expanse in the middle of the forest is something to see.

The Ride: At the entrance to the horse camp, turn left on Road 65 and follow it 0.2 mile. At the sign on the left side of the road, pick up the McClellan Meadows Trail #157, which is signed with blue diamonds on the trees. This trail is shared with bicycles, but lines of sight are usually long and the cyclists will normally be riding uphill toward you. (They come from Oldman Pass, ride up this trail to Road 65, then cruise down it and continue down the Falls Creek Trail #152.) The McClellan Meadows Trail runs downhill, crossing a bridge over Pete Gulch after 2 miles, then in another 0.5 mile crossing a bridge over a creek. In 0.6 mile after that you'll reach gravel Road 030 and a trail sign. Turn right on Road 030 and follow it 0.1 mile to where a sign on the right indicates the start of the Terminator Trail #159 (confusingly labeled the Snow Foot Trail #159 at this point). This will be your return route, but for now stay on Road 030 for another 0.3 mile. You'll see a trail sign for the Oldman Pass Trail #151, which goes off on the left to Oldman Pass trailhead in 1.8 mile. Tie your horses and follow the path on the opposite side of Road 030, which leads out into the impressive McClellan Meadows. After enjoying the view, ride back to the junction with the Terminator/Snow Foot Trail #159 and turn left on it. It goes steadily uphill, gaining 1,000 feet of elevation in 3.5 miles before it comes out in a big meadow at the edge of Road 65. Turn right on Road 65 and follow it 3 miles back to the horse camp.

McClellan Meadows is a vast wet prairie.

Reindeer lichen growing on a Douglas-fir branch

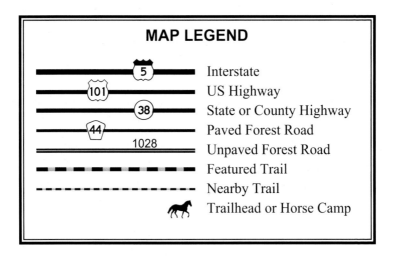

Grayback Mountain (Klickitat Wildlife Area)

Washington Dept. of Fish & Game

Grayback Mountain is located west of Goldendale, near Klickitat Canyon. You can camp at the adjacent Soda Springs Unit of the Klickitat Wildlife Area, which has a nice primitive campground that is open to horses. There are no single-track trails here, but cross-country travel is easy, and you'll find plenty of good riding on old logging/access roads. You'll also enjoy the beautiful oak and ponderosa pine forest and the open meadows of wildflowers in season. You can take in the panoramic views from the scenic overlook near Sheep Canyon and the summit of Grayback Mountain. Or you can explore the wildlife area's gently-rolling uplands near Klickitat Canyon. The Klickitat Wildlife Area is managed to provide habitat for black-tailed deer and wild turkeys and is very popular with game hunters in season.

Mt. Adams from Grayback Mountain.

Getting to Grayback Mountain

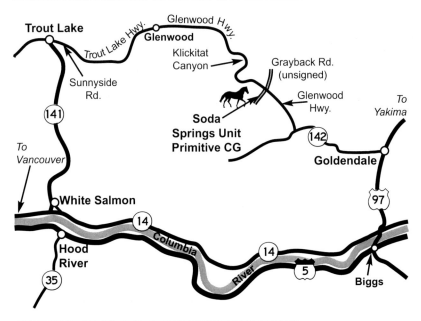

Grayback Mountain from the viewpoint near the camping area.

Grayback Mountain Area Trails

Trail	Difficulty	Elevation	Round Trip
Grayback Mountain Loop	Moderate	1,950-3,750	15 miles
Sheep Canyon Overlook	Moderate	1,950-2,450	10 miles
South of Glenwood Hwy.	Moderate	1,800-2,150	Varies

Soda Springs Unit Primitive Camp

Directions: From Trout Lake, go north on Mt. Adams Road. In 0.3 mile, turn right on Sunnyside Road. In 3.9 miles, go straight on Trout Lake Hwy. In 11.6 miles you'll reach Glenwood. About 0.7 mile past Glenwood, veer left at the Y on the Glenwood Hwy. toward Goldendale. Between mileposts 18 and 19, just as you climb out of Klickitat Canyon, turn right on a dirt road with a barbed-wire gate, directly across from unsigned Grayback Rd.
From Goldendale, follow Hwy. 142 west from Hwy. 97 for 11.7 miles and turn right on Glenwood Hwy. Follow it for 5.6 miles. Between mileposts 19 and 18, you'll see the unsigned Grayback Road going off to the right. Immediately turn left and drive through a barbed-wire gate.
All, if the barbed-wire gate is closed, please close it again after you drive through it. You'll find primitive campsites all along the next 0.6 mile of this road.

Elevation: 1,950 feet

Campsites: Primitive camping for many trailers along the 0.6-mile campground road. Horses are allowed in all sites. All sites are fairly level. No corrals, picnic tables or fire rings. Plenty of trees for highlining.

Facilities: Several outhouses are scattered along the campground road. Fires are not permitted from June 1 to October 30. Stock water may be available from a tank near the pond at the south end of the campground. If the water isn't on, you will have to bucket your stock water from the pond. If the water is not on, that means the grass is being rested for the year so please do not allow your horse to graze in the meadows near camp. Please pack out your trash and disperse your manure.

Permits: Discover Pass required

Season: May 1 through December 15

Contact: Washington Dept. of Fish and Wildlife, 360-902-2515,

Grayback Mountain Loop

Trailhead: Start at Soda Springs Unit primitive campground at Klickitat Wildlife Area

Length: 15 miles round trip

Elevation: 1,950 to 3,750 feet

Difficulty: Moderate -- big elevation change. A GPS and some navigation skills may be helpful, since none of the roads are signed or numbered

Footing: Hoof protection a must

Season: Early summer through fall

Permits: Discover Pass required

Facilities: Outhouses and stock water at the campground. Stock water is available on the trail.

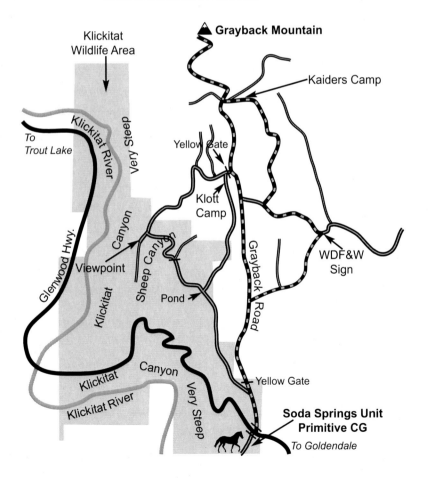

Highlights: This is a pretty strenuous ride for your horse, with steady uphill grades. In the last mile and a half before the summit, you'll want to stop a lot, both to rest your horse and to enjoy the splendid views. You'll see Mt. Adams, Mt. Hood, and Klickitat Canyon laid out before you, and from the summit you can see Mt. Rainier.

The Ride: Ride the campground road out to Glenwood Hwy. and continue on the unsigned Grayback Road directly across the highway. In 0.5 mile, the road to Sheep Canyon goes off to the left. Stay right, and in 0.1 mile you'll go thru a barbed-wire gate next to a yellow gate and cattle guard. In another mile, a road comes in on the right. This will be your return route if you make the loop. Stay to the left, and in 1.3 miles another road comes in on the right. Stay left. In 0.3 mile, you'll pass a road on the left blocked by a yellow gate. About 1.2 miles later you'll come to a 4-way junction just as you are leaving the trees behind. You'll take the road to the right on your return leg, but for now go straight on the main road and ride 1.6 miles to the summit to enjoy the spectacular views. Afterward, retrace your steps to the 4-way intersection. Turn left and ignore the road that almost immediately goes off to the left. In 0.3 mile you'll reach Kaiders Camp, a nice lunch spot with 2 derelict cabins and a water trough. Continue on this road and in 1.7 miles you'll intersect a gravel road. Going right takes you to Grayback Road, so turn left. After a mile you'll reach a large WDF&W sign that says the area is open for hunting. Make a hard right onto a road overgrown with grass (easy to follow, though) and it will take you to Grayback Road in 1.5 miles. Turn left to return to the campground.

Judy and Nine take in the view of Mt. Adams from the summit of Grayback Mountain.

Sheep Canyon Loop

Trailhead: Start at Soda Springs Unit primitive campground at Klicki-tat Wildlife Area

Length: 10 miles round trip

Elevation: 1,950 to 2,450 feet

Difficulty: Moderate -- a GPS and some navigation skills may be helpful, since none of the roads are signed or numbered

Footing: Hoof protection a must

Season: Early summer through fall

Permits: Discover Pass required

Facilities: Outhouses and stock water at the campground. Stock water is available on the trail.

Highlights: This trail explores the area south and west of Grayback Mountain, on the north side of Glenwood Hwy. Part of the trail parallels the rim of Klickitat Canyon, across which you'll enjoy a stunning view of Mt. Adams and Mt. Hood. The first several miles of the trail run through open grasslands, and then you'll enter a pretty forest of ponderosa pines, oaks, and Douglas-firs.

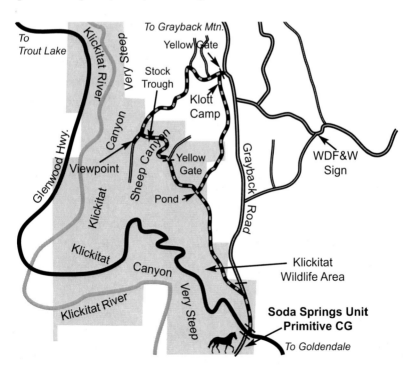

*Judy turns Nine around after enjoying the view
of Mt. Adams from the Sheep Canyon Overlook.*

The Ride: Follow the campground road out to Glenwood Hwy. Cross
the highway and begin riding up the unsigned Grayback Road. In 0.5
mile, veer left at the fork in the road. For the next 1.5 miles, you'll
have great views of Mt. Adams, a vista that gets better the higher you
ride. When you reach a pond on your left, the road forks again. Go
to the left. (The right leg will be your return route.) In another 0.8 mile
you'll go through a yellow gate and head downhill into Sheep Canyon.
About halfway up the other side, watch for a stock trough on your left
and a little way down the hillside. After watering your horse, continue
riding up the road. Just as you come up out of Sheep Canyon the road
forks. Take the left fork and ride uphill a short distance to a panoramic
viewpoint, then return to the junction and take the other fork. In the
next 1.9 miles, you'll see a couple of spur roads that go off on the left.
Stay right in each case, then turn right on a dirt road just before you
come to the yellow gate at Grayback Road. In 0.2 mile, you'll reach
Klott Camp, a good spot for a lunch break. Continue on this road for
another 1.5 miles and it will return you to the junction next to the pond.
Turn left here and retrace your steps back to your trailer.

South of Glenwood Hwy.

Trailhead: Start at Soda Springs unit primitive campground at Klicki-tat Wildlife Area

Length: Varies by route taken

Elevation: 1,800 to 2,150 feet

Difficulty: Moderate -- a GPS and some navigation skills may be helpful, since none of the roads are signed or numbered

Footing: Hoof protection recommended

Season: Early summer through fall

Permits: Discover Pass required

Facilities: Outhouses and stock water at the campground. No stock water on the trail.

Highlights: The portion of the Klickitat Wildlife Area that lies above Klickitat Canyon near the campground is fun to explore on horseback

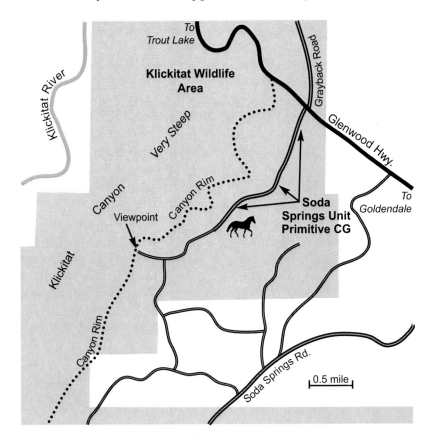

Judy rides Nine across a meadow toward a stand
of oak trees on the flats above the Klickitat River.

by following the cow trails and the few access roads, and by riding cross-country. The terrain is easy but the footing is rocky in places, and the low hills are so densely forested that you may have to go around them rather than over them. Because this area isn't very large and is bordered by the steep Klickitat Canyon on one side and boundary fences for the wildlife area on the other sides, you're not likely to get lost. So strap on your sense of adventure and go exploring!

The Ride: If you pick up the campground road and follow it southwest beyond the end of the camping area, in about a mile it will take you to a spectacular viewpoint from which you can see the Klickitat Canyon below you, Grayback Mountain to the north, and Mt. Adams and Mt. Hood to the west. You'll also have views of Mt. Adams from the upper portions of several of the meadows near the camp. Otherwise, you'll be exploring the meadows, the oak savannahs, and the forest on and around the wildlife area's low hills.

Whitestem frasera

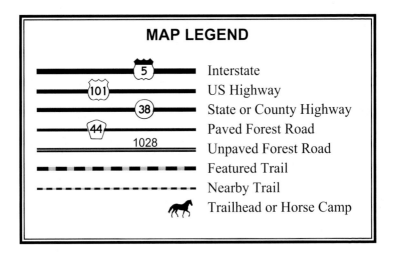

Green River Horse Camp

Gifford Pinchot National Forest

Green River Horse Camp lies between steep ridges in the valley carved by its namesake river. Two of the trails from the horse camp run into the Mt. St. Helens blast zone as they climb to the summits of the surrounding ridges and run along the ridge lines. These trails are steep and have some dropoffs, so they are not appropriate for green horses or riders, or for horses that are not well conditioned. However, if you make it to the ridge tops, the views are stunning.

The other trail out of camp is appropriate for all riders. It meanders with little elevation change along the Green River and through pretty second-growth and spectacular old-growth forest.

The area trails are shared with mountain bikes, but the lines of sight are fairly long, and much of the terrain is so steep and challenging that the bicyclists can't get up a real head of steam, even on their downhill runs.

Jean on Harley and Linda on Beamer, enjoying the view of Mt. St. Helens on the way to the top of Strawberry Mountain.

111

Getting to Green River

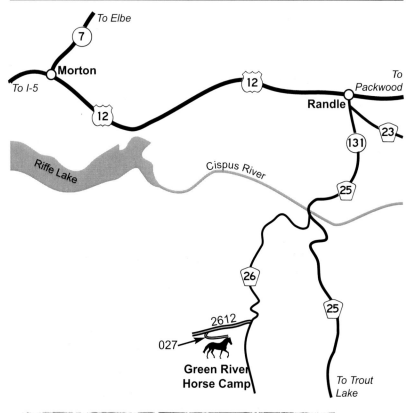

Tex and Beamer munch hay on their highline at Green River Horse Camp.

Green River Horse Camp

Directions: From I-5, take Exit 68 (Yakima/White Pass) and head east on Hwy. 12. After 48.5 miles, in Randle, head south on Hwy. 131/Cispus River Road, which soon becomes Forest Road 25. In about 8.5 miles you'll cross the Cispus River. Immediately veer right on Road 26, an unsigned one-lane paved road. In places the road has sunken and subsided, so it's quite rough but passable. (You'll pass a sign that says "Hazardous Road Conditions, Not Recommended for RV or Trailer Traffic" but the bumps and dips you'll encounter beyond this point are no worse than what you've already driven over, so just take it slow and you'll be fine.) Follow Road 26 for 12.4 miles and turn right on Road 2612 at a well-signed junction. Continue 1.5 miles, and when you reach a fork in the road, turn left on Road 027. In 0.6 mile, you'll reach the horse camp. **NOTE:** One of the roads to Green River Horse Camp was closed as of our publication date. Check with the Forest Service for access information before you make plans to visit.

Elevation: 2,900 feet

Campsites: 7 sites, all with highline poles and cables for 2 or 3 horses, plus fire pits and picnic tables. Five of the sites are pull-throughs that can accommodate 2 or 3 trailers.

Facilities: Vault toilet. Day-use parking for 3-5 trailers. Stock water is available from the Green River, but it's 0.1 mile from the nearest campsite -- too far to comfortably carry water -- so plan to walk your horse to the creek several times a day or bring your own stock water.

Permits: None

Season: Summer through fall

Contact: Mt. St. Helens NVM, 360-449-7800

Green River Area Trails

Trail	Difficulty	Elevation	Round Trip
Goat Mountain	Challenging	2,900-5,000	7 miles
Green River	Moderate	2,900-2,400	13.5 miles
Strawberry Mountain	Challenging	2,900-4,800	12.5 miles

Goat Mountain

Trailhead: Start at Green River Horse Camp
Length: 7 miles round trip
Elevation: 2,900 to 5,000 feet
Difficulty: Challenging -- big elevation gain in short distance, trail traverses very steep terrain
Footing: Hoof protection suggested
Season: Summer through fall
Permits: None
Facilities: Toilet at the horse camp. No stock water on the trail.

Highlights: Goat Mountain was aptly named, as the face of this mountain is extremely steep. Your horse will need to be in good condition, and if you don't like steep side hills this is not the trail for you. That said, intrepid riders who make it to the top of Goat Mountain and ride along the crest of the ridge for a short distance will be rewarded with breathtaking views of the Mt. St. Helens/Mt. Adams/Mt. Hood trifecta, as well as the St. Helens blast zone and Mt. Margaret Backcountry. You can even catch a glimpse of Mt. Rainier.

The Ride: Pick up the eastbound Green River Trail #213 on the east side of the turn-around area at the horse camp. In 0.7 mile you'll reach the junction with the Goat Mountain Trail #217. Turn left on it, and

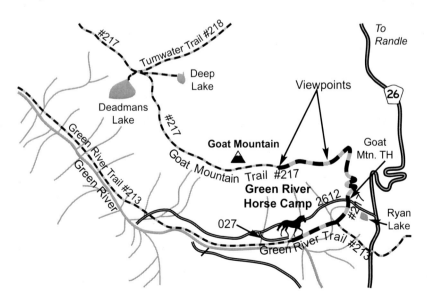

Jean and Linda ride Harley and Beamer near the top of Goat Mountain, with Mt. Margaret and Mt. St. Helens in the background.

in 0.4 mile you'll reach the Goat Mountain trailhead at Road 2612. The trail continues to the left of the trailhead parking area. From here the trail switchbacks up the very steep and heavily-wooded face of Goat Mountain, gaining 1,500 feet of elevation in 1.7 miles. When you come out on the top of the ridge, you'll have a nice view of Mt. Rainier just to the right of the trail. Continue along the top of the ridge for 0.6 mile, to a large open area that offers a panoramic view of Mt. St. Helens and the blast zone, as well as Mt. Adams, Mt. Hood, and the Mt. Margaret Backcountry. This is a good place to turn around. The trail beyond this point is not horse friendly, as it enters the blast zone and traverses the very steep and exposed face of Goat Mountain while the ground drops sharply away to the river valley 2,000 feet below. We cannot recommend continuing beyond the viewpoint.

The trail beyond the viewpoint on Goat Mountain is steep and exposed.

Green River

Trailhead: Start at Green River Horse Camp

Length: 3.5 miles round trip to the waterfall, or 13.5 miles round trip to the Vanson Ridge Trail junction, or 18 miles round trip to Road 2500

Elevation: 2,900 to 2,800 feet to the waterfall, or 2,900 to 2,400 feet to the Vanson Ridge Trail junction, or 2,900 to 1,900 feet to Road 2500

Difficulty: Moderate

Footing: Hoof protection suggested

Season: Summer through fall

Permits: None

Facilities: Toilet at the horse camp. Stock water is available on the trail.

Highlights: Compared to the strenuous and challenging Goat Mountain and Strawberry Mountain trails, this trail is a relaxing walk in the park. This stretch of the Green River Trail doesn't offer any panoramic views, but the forest is beautiful and quite varied, with second-growth forest in the first 4 miles of the trail and massive old growth trees after that. There's even a waterfall. While there are a few bridges and small creeks to cross, the riding is otherwise easy, with smooth footing and little elevation change. The shade is welcome on a hot day.

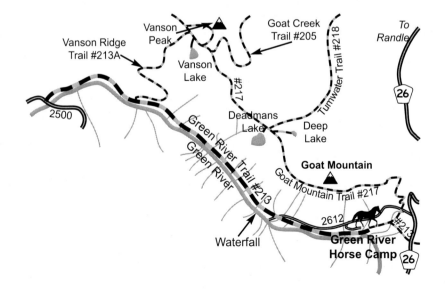

Green River Falls

The Ride: Pick up the westbound Green River Trail #213 on the south side of the horse camp's turn-around area. The trail roughly follows the river, at times moving away from it and at times running along the bank. After 1.5 miles, you'll cross gravel Road 2612, and 0.3 mile later you'll come to a pretty double falls where the river drops over a basalt outcropping. In another 0.7 mile, the trail goes through a meadow -- look for the signpost on the far side to indicate where the trail continues. A mile after that, the trail forks. The main trail goes to the right, but if you detour to the left you'll find a nice riverside watering spot for the horses. Return to the main trail, and you'll soon enter the old-growth section of the trail, where immense firs, hemlocks, and cedars create a magical environment. (Surely there are fairy folk living beneath the oxalis or in that hollow tree!)   The next 2.8 miles to the junction with the Vanson Ridge Trail #213A go by in a blink. From here you can continue 2.5 miles farther to the end of the trail at Weyerhauser Road 2500, or at any point you can retrace your steps to return to the horse camp.

Jean and Linda ride Harley and Beamer among the old-growth trees on the Green River Trail.

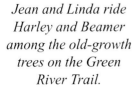

Strawberry Mountain

Trailhead: Start at Green River Horse Camp

Length: 9 miles round trip to the Strawberry Trail, or 12.5 miles round trip to the Strawberry Mountain lookout

Elevation: 2,900 to 4,800 feet

Difficulty: Challenging -- big elevation gains, steep terrain. May be difficult if trail has not been maintained.

Footing: Hoof protection suggested

Season: Summer through fall

Permits: None

Facilities: Toilet at the horse camp. Stock water is available on the trail.

Highlights: East of the horse camp, the Green River Trail leaves the river and travels steeply uphill to the Strawberry Mountain Trail #220, which runs along the spine of Strawberry Mountain. The trail to the top of the ridge is easier than the Goat Mountain Trail because the terrain isn't quite as steep. However, your horse will need to be in good condition, and this is not a trail for inexperienced horses or riders. When you reach the Strawberry Mountain Trail, which was developed

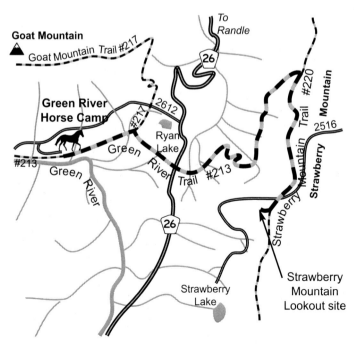

*Linda on Beamer and Jean on Harley, as they head up
the Green River Trail toward Strawberry Mountain.*

by miners before 1895, turn south on it and ride to the site of the old
Strawberry Mountain fire lookout to enjoy the panoramic views.

The Ride: Pick up the eastbound Green River Trail #213 on the east
side of the horse camp turn-around area. In 0.7 mile, you'll reach the
junction with the Goat Mountain Trail #217. Veer right to stay on the
Green River Trail. The trail begins climbing steeply, and in 0.5 mile
it reaches a dirt road. Turn left and follow the dirt road uphill. In 0.1
mile, you'll reach Road 26. Cross it and pick up the trail on the other
side. In the next 1.2 miles, you'll cross several small creeks running
across the trail, then come out on a dirt road. Turn left and follow it.
After 0.3 mile this road (which was very overgrown with alders when
we rode it) becomes a single-track that continues straight ahead
through a small ravine, then becomes a road again. In 0.2 mile, the
Green River Trail veers off the dirt road to the left and becomes a single track again. From here the trail traverses the ridge and heads
steadily uphill for another 1.5 miles to the junction with the Strawberry Trail #220. Turn right on the Strawberry Trail, and in 1.4 miles
you'll cross gravel Road 2516. In another 0.3 mile a short spur trail
on the right will take you to the site of the old fire lookout on Strawberry Mountain, where you'll find an excellent view of Mt. St. Helens.

Indian paintbrush

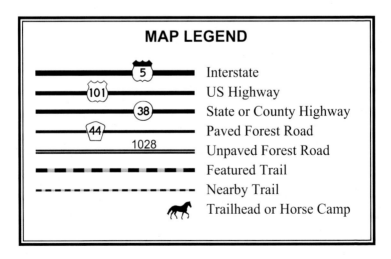

Kalama Horse Camp

Gifford Pinchot National Forest

There is something for every rider at Kalama Horse Camp, from easy trails along the Kalama River to challenging climbs that traverse steep ridges and offer impressive views of Mt. St. Helens. Evidence of volcanic activity is everywhere. Several of the area trails run on huge primeval lahar deposits (deep mud flows that were a slurry of rock and ash). Others run across ancient lava flows, and some cross mud flows from the 1980 eruption. The terrain is very rocky, so hoof protection is a must.

The Kalama River was named after John Kalama, a Hawaiian who came to the Pacific Northwest to work for the Hudsons Bay Company. He married a local native and settled near the mouth of the Kalama River, which was named after him after he drowned there.

Mt. St. Helens from the Toutle Trail above McBride Lake.
The lake has been largely silted in since the 1980 eruption,
and is now mostly overgrown with alders.

Getting to Kalama Horse Camp

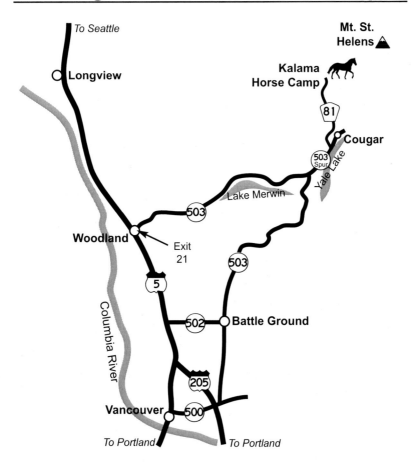

Kalama Area Trails

Trail	Difficulty	Elevation	Round Trip
Blue Lake Loop	Moderate	2,100-3,400	12.5 miles
Cinnamon Loop	Challenging	2,100-3,950	14 miles
Fossil Loop	Challenging	2,100-3,600	12.5 miles
Kalama Ski/Toutle Lp--Short	Easy	2,100-2,550	4 miles
Toutle/Kalama Ski Lp--Long	Challenging	2,000-3,500	13 miles

Kalama Horse Camp

Directions: From I-5, take the Woodland/Cougar exit (Exit 21) and head east on Hwy. 503/Lewis River Road, toward Cougar. In 23 miles, Hwy. 503 turns sharply to the right. Go straight on the Hwy. 503-Spur. In 4.3 miles, turn left on Road 81 (Road 8100) at the sign for the Kalama Recreation Area. Drive 8.5 miles to a junction, turn right to stay on Road 81, and continue 0.2 mile to the campground.

Elevation: 2,100 feet

Campsites: 26 sites, all with fire pits and picnic tables. 18 sites are pull-throughs with 4-horse corrals and room for 2 vehicles. 8 sites (all located on the interiors of the two campground loops) have 2-horse corrals and room for one vehicle. Several sites are group sites with room for extra vehicles and horses.

Facilities: Each campground loop has a toilet, stock water trough, manure bin, and accessible mounting ramp. An enclosed group shelter with a woodburning stove is located in the horse camp. The day-use area has parking for 8-10 trailers, stock water, toilet, accessible mounting ramp, stock loading ramp, and picnic table.

Permits: Camping fee; Northwest Forest Pass required for day use

Season: Summer through fall

Contact: Mt. St. Helens National Volcanic Monument, 360-449-7800

Magic relaxes in his corral at Kalama Horse Camp.

Blue Lake Loop

Trailhead: Start at the day-use area at Kalama Horse Camp
Length: 12.5 miles round trip
Elevation: 2,100 to 3,400 feet
Difficulty: Moderate
Footing: Hoof protection a must
Season: Summer through fall
Permits: Camping fee, no fee for day-use parking
Facilities: Toilets, stock water, manure bins, accessible mounting ramps, and day-use parking for 8-10 trailers. Stock water is available on the trail.

Highlights: This pleasant loop offers filtered views of Mt. St. Helens, with no steep drop-offs and only a moderate elevation gain. However, the Kalama Ski Trail and the Toutle Trail near Blue Lake are very rocky. The Blue Horse Trail from Road 81 to the junction with the Kalama Ski Trail runs through beautiful old-growth forest and offers great footing for the horses, making it easily the nicest stretch of trail in the area. We recommend riding the loop clockwise so you'll save this delightful stretch of trail for last.

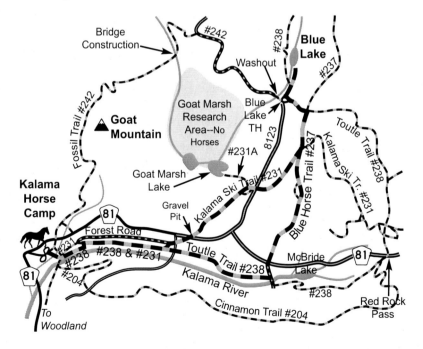

The Ride: From the day-use area, pick up the Toutle Trail #238. In the first 0.1 mile the Cinnamon Trail #204 departs to the right and then in 100 feet the Kalama Ski Trail #231 goes to the left. Stay on the Toutle Trail, and in 1.9 miles turn left at the junction where the Kalama Ski Trail splits off.   Follow the Kalama Ski Trail, and in 0.4 mile you'll cross gravel Road 81. The trail runs through an old gravel pit and continues on the far side. In 0.9 mile, you'll pass the junction with the Goat Marsh Trail #231A, then in 0.2 mile you'll cross Road 8123. One mile after that, you'll come to the 4-way intersection of the Kalama Ski and Blue Horse Trails. Turn left on the Blue Horse Trail #237 and in 0.3 mile you'll reach the 4-way intersection of the Blue Horse and Toutle Trails. Turn left on the Toutle Trail. In another 0.3 mile the trail to the Blue Lake trailhead goes off to the left. Stay right, and in 100 feet a connector trail to the Fossil Trail goes to the left. Veer right and follow the trail 0.5 mile across the mud flow to Blue Lake. When the Toutle Trail turns left and crosses the creek, stay right. The last 100 feet of the trail is too rocky for horses, so you'll have to tie them and continue on foot to see Blue Lake. Retrace your steps to the 4-way junction of the Blue Horse and Toutle Trails. Turn right on the Blue Horse Trail and follow it 2.5 miles (a very pretty, horse-friendly stretch of trail) to gravel Road 81. Cross Road 81 and continue on the blocked-off dirt road on the other side. In 0.3 mile you'll come to the Toutle Trail, just before the dirt road crosses the Kalama River. Turn right on the Toutle Trail and follow it 3.7 miles back to the horse camp.

Lydia and Magic enjoy a great view of Mt. St. Helens on the Kalama Ski Trail, on the way to Blue Lake.

Cinnamon Loop

Trailhead: Start at the day-use area at Kalama Horse Camp

Length: 14 miles round trip

Elevation: 2,100 to 3,950 feet, with a cumulative elevation gain of 2,950 feet

Difficulty: Challenging -- steep and rocky trail, some steep side slopes

Footing: Hoof protection recommended

Season: Summer through fall

Permits: Camping fee, no fee for day-use parking

Facilities: Toilets, stock water, manure bins, accessible mounting ramps, and day-use parking for 8-10 trailers. Stock water is available on the trail.

Highlights: This trail is challenging, with big elevation gains and some traverses of steep side hills. But experienced riders on well-conditioned horses will enjoy panoramic views of Mt. St. Helens (and in one spot Mt. Adams, too) from along the Cinnamon Trail.

The Ride: From the day-use area, pick up the Toutle Trail #238. In 0.1 mile, turn right on the Cinnamon Trail #204. It heads steadily uphill, gaining nearly 2,000 feet of elevation in the first 3.3 miles. For the next 4 miles the trail runs along the ridge below Cinnamon Peak, losing 600 feet of elevation, then regaining 500 feet. There are occasional steep side slopes to traverse as you climb the ridge and ride along it. Then the trail descends for a mile toward Red Rock Pass, losing 650 feet of elevation. Just before reaching Red Rock Pass, the

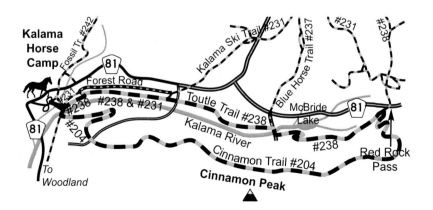

Mt. St. Helens and Mt. Adams, seen from the Cinnamon Trail.

trail intersects with the Toutle Trail #238. Turn left on the Toutle Trail and follow it 5.7 miles back to the horse camp, gradually losing another 1,000 feet of elevation. The 2-mile stretch of the Toutle Trail that runs from Red Rock Pass to McBride Lake features stretches of narrow trail and steep dropoffs as the trail traverses a ridge covered with old-growth noble firs. Once you get past McBride Lake, the trail is easy, with wide tread and no dropoffs as it travels beside the beautiful Kalama River. Continue on the Toutle Trail another 3.7 miles to return to the horse camp.

Lydia and Magic head back to the horse camp on the Toutle Trail.

Fossil Loop

Trailhead: Start at the day-use area at Kalama Horse Camp

Length: 12.5 miles round trip

Elevation: 2,100 to 3,600 feet, with a cumulative elevation gain of 3,300 feet

Difficulty: Challenging -- steep and rocky trail, some steep side slopes

Footing: Hoof protection recommended

Season: Summer through fall

Permits: Camping fee, no fee for day-use parking

Facilities: Toilets, stock water, manure bins, accessible mounting ramps, and day-use parking for 8-10 trailers. Stock water is available on the trail.

Highlights: This loop features big elevation changes, some steep side hills, and rocky footing. These challenges are offset by the tremendous variety in scenery and terrain and by the beauty of the forest, including some of the largest old-growth noble firs in the world. We were

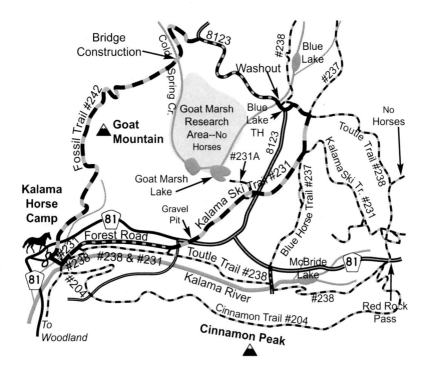

*Theresa rides Breeze on the Fossil Loop Trail
on the lower flank of Goat Mountain.*

unable to complete the entire loop because the bridge over Cold Spring
Creek was under construction, but the information below is from
sources we believe to be accurate.

The Ride: From the day-use area at Kalama Horse Camp, pick up the
Fossil Trail #242. You'll come to several unsigned junctions as you
head out, but stay to the right because the trails on the left all return to
camp. In 0.2 mile, you'll cross Road 81. The trail soon begins climbing, following switchbacks steeply up and across the face of Goat
Mountain. It then descends to an abandoned forest road and follows
it uphill to the closed segment of Road 8123. Turn right on Road 8123
and follow it to the mud flow near Blue Lake. When you reach the
junction with the Toutle Trail #238, veer right on it. Shortly afterward, you'll come to a 4-way junction of the Toutle and Blue Horse
Trails. Turn right on the Blue Horse Trail #237 and continue 0.3 mile.
At the 4-way junction of the Blue Horse and Kalama Ski Trails, turn
right on the Kalama Ski Trail #231 and follow it 4.5 miles back to the
horse camp. About 0.4 mile after crossing Road 81 you'll have the
option of veering right on a rocky forest road or veering left to reach
the combined Kalama Ski and Toutle Trails. Either way will take you
back to the horse camp.

Kalama Ski/Toutle Loop--Short

Trailhead: Start at the day-use area at Kalama Horse Camp
Length: 4 miles
Elevation: 2,100 to 2,550 feet
Difficulty: Easy
Footing: Hoof protection recommended -- rocky trail
Season: Summer through fall
Permits: Camping fee, no fee for day-use parking
Facilities: Toilets, stock water, manure bins, accessible mounting ramps, and day-use parking for 8-10 trailers. Stock water is available on the trail.

Highlights: If you'd like a short, relatively easy loop, this is the trail for you. There are several unsigned user-created trails near camp that branch off from the official trails, so riding this loop will help you get oriented to the trails and trail junctions near the horse camp. The portion of the loop that runs along the old forest road is actually not an official trail so its junctions are not signed, but it is well traveled and easy to follow.

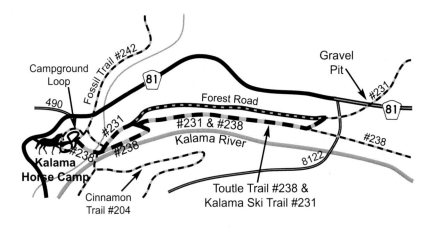

The Ride: Three trails depart from the day-use area. The Fossil Trail #242 heads off on the left toward Goat Mountain. The 0.9-mile Campground Loop goes to the right and makes a loop around the campground. You'll take the Toutle Trail #238 (pronounced TOO-tul), which departs in the middle. In 0.1 mile the Cinnamon Trail #204 goes off to the right. Stay left, and in another 100 feet you'll come to a junction with the Kalama Ski Trail #231. Turn left on the Kalama Ski Trail. In about 0.1 mile you'll reach an unsigned junction where a user-created trail goes to the left toward the Fossil Trail, but you'll go to the right and across a dry wash. In another 0.6 mile the trail forks again. Veer left here, and the route will run eastward along a rocky forest road for 1.2 miles to a junction with the Kalama Ski Trail. Turn right on it, and in 0.1 mile turn right again on the combined Toutle/Kalama Ski Trail. Follow it westward along the river, and in 1.1 mile the Kalama Ski Trail splits off to the right. Stay to the left and follow the Toutle Trail down a steep embankment and along the river-bank for 0.8 mile back to the horse camp.

Lydia and Magic on the Toutle Trail
near Kalama Horse Camp.

Toutle/Kalama Ski Loop--Long

Trailhead: Start at the day-use area at Kalama Horse Camp

Length: 13 miles round trip

Elevation: 2,000 to 3,500 feet

Difficulty: Moderate to McBride Lake, challenging after that because the trail is narrow and traverses steep side slopes near McBride Lake, and some stretches are very rocky

Footing: Hoof protection is a must

Season: Summer through fall

Permits: Camping fee, no fee for day-use parking

Facilities: Toilets, stock water, manure bins, accessible mounting ramps, and day-use parking for 8-10 trailers. Stock water is available on the trail.

Highlights: The elevation changes on this trail are small compared to others in the area, but it does have some challenges: steep dropoffs along the trail above McBride Lake, and very rocky trail at Red Rock Pass and on the Kalama Ski Trail.   You are rewarded for the challenging bits, however, with eye-popping views of Mt. St. Helens from the trail above McBride Lake and from the lava flows at Red Rock Pass. And as you return to the horse camp on the Kalama Ski Trail, don't forget to look behind you at the mountain views!

The Ride: From the day-use area, pick up the Toutle Trail #238. In the first 0.1 mile, the Cinnamon Trail #204 departs to the right (you'll stay left) and then in 100 feet the Kalama Ski Trail #231 goes to the

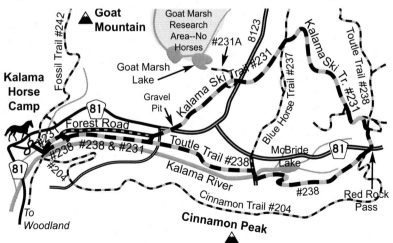

Lydia rides Magic across the lava flow at Red Rock Pass.

left (you'll stay right). Follow the Toutle Trail for 3.5 miles to a dirt road. If you turn left on it you'll be on the Blue Horse Trail #237. Instead, turn right on the dirt road, cross over the Kalama River, and pick up the Toutle Trail again on the other side. The going soon gets more challenging as the trail traverses a steep ridge above McBride Lake. The views of Mt. St. Helens in this stretch are spectacular. In 2.3 miles you'll reach Red Rock Pass trailhead. Continue on the Toutle Trail, across the lava flow, for 0.6 mile. You'll come to an unsigned junction where the Toutle Trail goes to the right and the Kalama Ski Trail #231 goes to the left. Turn left on the Kalama Ski Trail (marked with blue diamonds) and follow it for 2.3 miles. In this section the trail crosses a mud flow with huge boulders. It's easy to lose the trail here, so be sure to work your way across the flow rather than up it. When you reach the junction with the Blue Horse Trail, cross it and continue on the Kalama Ski Trail. (The sign indicating it's 3.75 miles to Kalama Horse Camp via the Blue Lake Trail is wrong -- it's more like 6 miles. It's 4.5 miles back to camp if you stay on the Kalama Ski Trail.) In 1 mile you'll cross Road 8123, then in another mile you'll cross Road 81. Continue another 2.4 miles on the Kalama Ski Trail to return to the horse camp. Note that about 0.4 mile after crossing Road 81, you'll have the option of veering right on a rocky forest road or veering left to reach the combined Kalama Ski and Toutle Trails. Either route will take you back to the horse camp.

Queens cup

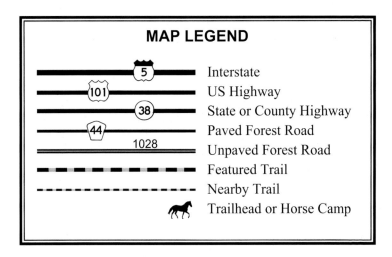

Keenes Horse Camp

Gifford Pinchot National Forest

Keenes Horse Camp (pronounced KEY-nuss) was named for Keenes Meade, a Forest Service mule packer. Located on the north side of Mt. Adams, the camp provides access to a wide variety of outstanding trails. The soil is volcanic pumice, so the trails can get pretty dusty by late summer, but they are never slippery after rain. And the sights you'll see on these trails are amazing! You can ride lower-elevation forested loops of varying lengths, take in the 360-degree panorama from the summit of Green Mountain, or enjoy beautiful meadows, a waterfall, small lakes, and jaw-dropping mountain views in the Mt. Adams Wilderness. No matter what kind of riding you like, there's something for you to enjoy at Keenes Horse Camp.

Mt. Adams from the Muddy Meadows Trail
near Keenes Horse Camp.

Getting to Keenes Horse Camp

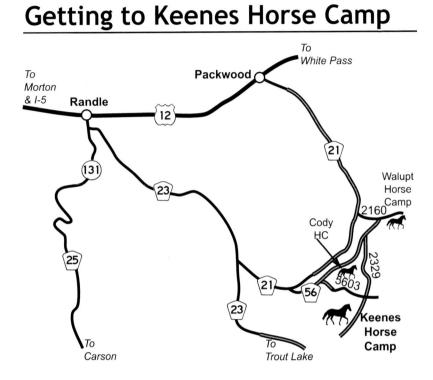

Riders care for their horses on a highline at Keenes Horse Camp.

Keenes Horse Camp

Directions: From I-5, take Exit 68 (Morton/Yakima) and head east on Hwy. 12.   In 48.5 miles, in Randle, turn right on Hwy. 131.   When the road makes a Y in 1 mile, veer left on Road 23. Follow it for 17.7 miles, then turn left on Road 21. Drive 4.7 miles and turn right on Road 56. From here on, signs point the way to Keenes Horse Camp. Continue for 3 miles on Road 56, which is paved at first, then gravel. Turn right on Road 5603, which is gravel at first, then paved. Follow it for 5.2 miles and turn right on gravel Road 2329. In 2.1 miles you'll arrive at the entrance to Keenes sites 1-8 (the "new" campground) on the right. The entrance to Keenes sites 9-13 (the "old" campground) is 0.1 mile farther ahead on the right. **NOTE:** As of our publication date, Road 23 was closed due to a washout. Check with the Forest Service for access information before you make plans to visit.

Elevation: 4,350 feet

Campsites: 13 sites with highline posts, picnic tables, and fire rings. Sites 1-8 are in the "new" loop; most are pull-throughs and all can accommodate larger rigs. Sites 9-13 are in the "old" loop and are designed for smaller trailers. Several sites in both loops are large enough for 2+ trailers.

Facilities: Toilets, manure bins, stock water from a trough, accessible mounting ramp. Day use parking is in the "old" loop.

Permits: Camping fee

Season: Summer through fall

Contact: Cowlitz Valley Ranger District, 360-497-1100

Keenes Area Trails

Trail	Difficulty	Elevation	Round Trip
Green Mountain	Moderate	4,000-5,100	8.5 miles
Horseshoe Lake Loop	Moderate	4,000-4,400	4.5 miles
Killen Cr./Muddy Mdws. Lp.	Moderate	4,250-6,100	13 miles
Lava Spring	Moderate	4,300-5,250	12-15.5 miles
Midway Meadows Loop	Moderate	3,750-4,400	12 miles

Green Mountain

Trailhead: Start at Keenes Horse Camp

Length: 8.5 miles round trip

Elevation: 4,000 to 5,100 feet

Difficulty: Moderate -- steep section, creek crossing

Footing: Hoof protection recommended

Season: Summer through fall

Permits: Camping fee; no fee for day use

Facilities: Toilets, stock water, manure bins, and day-use parking for several trailers at the horse camp. Stock water is available on the trail.

Highlights: The trail to Green Mountain is mostly easy, but the last two miles before you reach the summit of Green Mountain are fairly strenuous. The views from the summit are panoramic. On a clear day, this former fire lookout site provides views of Mt. Adams, Mt. St. Helens, Mt. Rainier, and the Goat Rocks. Stupendous!

The Ride: Pick up the Keenes Trail #120 next to the day-use parking area in the old campground loop. In 0.9 mile, turn left on the High Lakes Trail #116 toward Horseshoe Lake. In 0.2 mile, turn left again

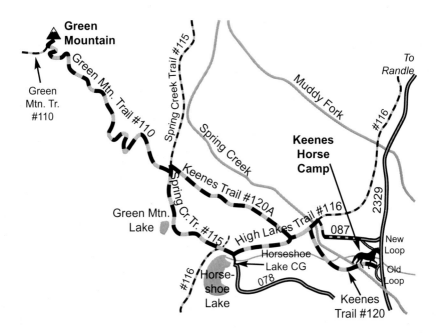

Nancy, Barb, Donna, and Kim on Will, Riata, Zoey, and Tex, at the top of Green Mountain with Mt. Rainier on the horizon at left.

at an unsigned junction to stay on the High Lakes Trail. In 0.4 mile you'll come to another junction. Horseshoe Lake Campground is to the left, so turn right. In 0.1 mile you'll reach Horseshoe Lake. Its boggy shore is not safe for horses, so continue along the trail. Almost immediately you'll come to an unsigned trail on the right. Ignore it and continue straight ahead, and in another 200 feet you'll come to a signed junction where the High Lakes Trail goes to the left. Go straight on the Spring Creek Trail #115. In 1.6 miles, turn left on the Green Mountain Trail #110. In 0.2 mile it begins to climb, heading steadily uphill for 1.8 miles. Near the top the Green Mountain Trail turns left toward Road 5601, but you'll go straight and in 0.2 mile you'll arrive at the summit of Green Mountain. After enjoying the views, follow the Green Mountain Trail back down and turn left on the Spring Creek Trail. In 100 feet, turn right on the Keenes Trail #120A and follow it for 1.1 mile, turning right when you reach the un- signed junction with the High Lakes Trail. In another 0.2 mile, when the Keenes Trail #120 veers to the right near the bank of Spring Creek, stay left and cross the creek. On the other side, immediately turn right on an unsigned trail. It will take you to Road 087 in 0.1 mile. Veer left on Road 087 and follow it 0.3 mile, then turn right to enter the "new" Keenes campground loop.

Horseshoe Lake Loop

Trailhead: Start at Keenes Horse Camp

Length: 4.5 miles round trip

Elevation: 4,000 to 4,400 feet

Difficulty: Moderate -- creek crossing

Footing: Hoof protection suggested

Season: Summer through fall

Permits: Camping fee; no fee for day use

Facilities: Toilets, stock water, manure bins, and day-use parking for several trailers at the horse camp. Stock water is available on the trail.

Highlights: If you're looking for a short, relaxing, low-elevation trail, this is the ride for you. It runs through mixed-conifer forest with a dense understory of huckleberry, bear grass, lupine, and white rhododendron, past burbling streams, and to the shore of pretty Horseshoe Lake. Horseshoe Lake's shore is boggy and muddy, so it's not safe to water your horse there.

The Ride: Pick up the Keenes Trail #120 next to the day-use parking area in the old campground loop. In 0.9 mile, turn left on the High

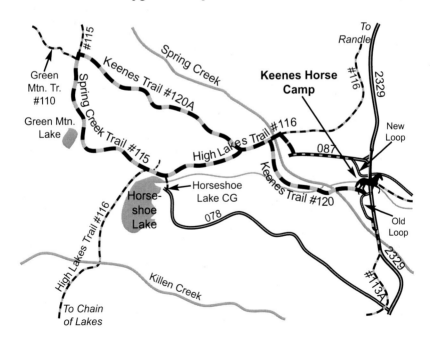

Lakes Trail #116 toward Horseshoe Lake. In 0.2 mile, turn left at an unsigned junction to stay on the High Lakes Trail. In 0.4 mile you'll come to another junction. Horseshoe Lake Campground is to the left, so turn right. In 0.1 mile you'll reach Horseshoe Lake. Continue along the trail and almost immediately you'll come to an unsigned trail on the right. Ignore it and continue straight ahead, and in another 200 feet you'll come to a signed junction where the High Lakes Trail goes to the left. Go straight on the Spring Creek Trail #115. In 1.6 miles, the Green Mountain Trail #110 goes off to the left. Continue straight for 100 feet and turn right on the Keenes Trail #120A. Follow it 1.1 miles, then turn left on the High Lakes Trail. In 0.2 mile, near the bank of Spring Creek, the Keenes Trail #120 goes off to the right. Stay to the left and cross Spring Creek, then immediately turn right on an unsigned trail. It will take you to Road 087 in 0.1 mile. Turn left on Road 087 and in 0.3 mile turn right on the gravel road that will take you into the "new" loop at Keenes Horse Camp.

Bonus Ride: From Horseshoe Lake, turn left on the High Lakes Trail #116 and follow it 3 miles to reach the Chain of Lakes, a string of lakes arrayed along the trail like beads on a necklace. The round trip is 9.5 miles, with elevations of 3,700 to 4,400 feet. When we were there the bridge over Adams Fork was washed out. Before you ride, contact the Forest Service to make sure the trail is passable.

Tex enjoys the view of Horseshoe Lake.

Killen Creek/Muddy Mdws. Loop

Trailhead: Start at Keenes Horse Camp

Length: 13 miles round trip

Elevation: 4,250 to 6,100 feet

Difficulty: Moderate, though a steep section of the Killen Creek Trail is somewhat challenging

Footing: Hoof protection recommended; trail is rocky in places

Season: Summer through fall

Permits: Camping fee; no fee for day use

Facilities: Toilets, stock water, manure bins, and day-use parking for several trailers at the horse camp. Stock water is available on the trail.

Highlights: This ride will give your horse a real workout, as it gains almost 2,000 feet of elevation, and in places the Killen Creek Trail is steep enough that its water bars seem like stairs. The payoff: stunning views of Mt. Adams from several vantage points, so close you can al-

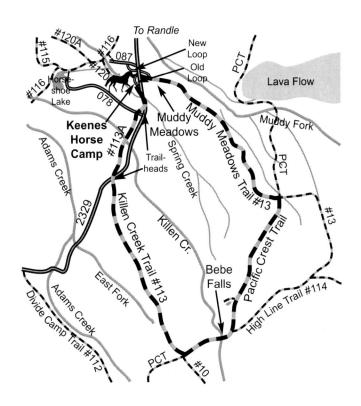

Barb on Riata, Donna on Zoey, and Nancy on Will,
on the Killen Creek Trail with Mt. Adams in the background.

most touch it. You'll also have panoramic views of Mt. Rainier, the
Goat Rocks, and other nearby mountains. Beautiful!

The Ride: Pick up Trail #113A across from campsite 13 in the "old"
loop. In 0.1 mile, it comes out on Road 2329 and runs along it to the
right for a short distance to the Killen Creek hiker parking area, then
veers off the road to the right on a single-track trail. About 1.7 miles
later, the trail crosses Road 2329 at another trailhead and becomes the
Killen Creek Trail #113. Then the trail heads steadily uphill. After 2.5
miles you'll get a spectacular view of Mt. Adams from a large meadow
beside the trail. As you ride the next mile to the junction with the PCT,
you'll have more views of Mt. Adams from the trail. Turn left on the
PCT. The trail begins to gently descend, providing views of Mt.
Rainier and the Ghost Rocks. After 1.1 mile you'll cross Killen Creek.
Detour to the left here to see pretty Bebe Falls. About 0.2 mile later,
the High Line Trail #114 goes off to the right. Stay left on the PCT,
and in another 0.7 mile detour to the left to a pretty little unnamed lake
with a view of Mt. Adams. In another 1.7 miles, turn left at the junction with the Muddy Meadows Trail #13. Follow it steadily downhill
for 3.5 miles to Muddy Meadows, with its jaw-dropping views of Mt.
Adams. In 0.1 mile, you'll come to the Muddy Meadows hiker trailhead, and 0.4 mile later you'll be back at the horse camp.

Lava Spring

Trailhead: Start at Keenes Horse Camp

Length: 12 miles round trip to Lava Spring, 13 miles round trip if you continue along the lava flow, and 15.5 miles round trip if you ride to Road 5603

Elevation: 4,300 to 5,250 feet

Difficulty: Moderate -- bridges, some moderately steep sections

Footing: Hoof protection recommended

Season: Summer through fall

Permits: Camping fee; no fee for day use

Facilities: Toilets, stock water, manure bins, and day-use parking for several trailers at the horse camp. Stock water is available on the trail.

Highlights: This out-and-back ride follows the Muddy Meadows Trail to the PCT, then runs along the PCT to Lava Spring, where a steady stream of water gushes out of the base of an impressive lava flow. Along the way you'll get a stunning view of Mt. Adams from

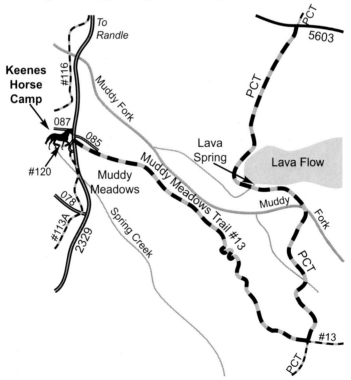

Donna on Zoey, Barb on Riata, and Nancy on Will,
riding along the lava flow just past Lava Spring.

Muddy Meadows, see a stand of "ghost trees" still standing after a long-ago fire, cross a bridge over the raging Muddy Fork, and catch glimpses of Mt. Adams over the top of the lava flow.

The Ride: Pick up the Muddy Meadows Trail #13 across Road 2329 from the entrance to the new loop at Keenes Horse Camp. In 0.5 mile you'll be at Muddy Meadows, with its picture-postcard views of Mt. Adams. Continue another 3.1 miles to reach the PCT, during which you will gain 850 feet of elevation. Turn left on the PCT and follow it downhill for 2.5 miles, during which you will steadily lose 800 feet of elevation. After you've been on the PCT for about 0.8 mile, you'll ride through an old burn area, its dead trees silvery against the sky above and juvenile trees growing up to take their place. In another 0.8 mile you'll cross the bridge over the Muddy Fork, and in another 0.3 mile you'll catch your first glimpse of the large lava flow. Ride 0.6 mile farther to reach Lava Spring. (You can't get your horses to the water without damaging the spring, so bring a collapsible bucket for them and enjoy a lunch stop here.)   If you continue another 0.5 mile you'll be riding along the edge of the lava flow. Impressive! After that you can continue on to Road 5603 or retrace your steps to return to your trailer.

Midway Meadows Loop

Trailhead: Start at Keenes Horse Camp

Length: 12 miles round trip

Elevation: 3,750 to 4,400 feet

Difficulty: Moderate, with one rather challenging creek crossing

Footing: Hoof protection recommended

Season: Summer through fall

Permits: Camping fee; no fee for day use

Facilities: Toilets, stock water, manure bins, and day-use parking for several trailers at the horse camp. Stock water is available on the trail.

Highlights: This trail doesn't have spectacular mountain views, but it does showcase a variety of forest ecosystems: it travels through mixed-conifer forest with huckleberries and bear grass in the understory, through arid lodgepole forest, through stands of Douglas-fir (including some old growth) with shade so dense almost nothing grows beneath, and through tree plantations logged and replanted some 20 years ago. Midway Meadows is a nice place for your horse to graze

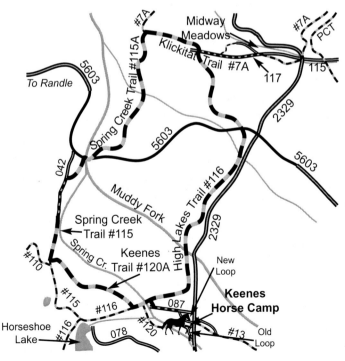

while you have lunch. And other than the fairly steep downhill section at the north end of the Spring Creek Trail, the terrain and footing
invite trotting or gaiting.

The Ride: Ride through the new loop at the horse camp and turn left
on Road 087. At the end of the road in 0.3 mile, pick up the single
track on the right side of the road. In 0.1 mile turn right on the High
Lakes Trail #116. After 0.9 mile the trail goes down a steep and rocky
bank and crosses Muddy Fork, so filled with glacial silt that you can't
see the bottom, then goes steeply up the other side. In 1.6 miles you'll
cross paved Road 5603, and 1.1 mile later you'll arrive at the junction
with the Klickitat Trail #7A at dirt Road 117. The Klickitat Trail goes
to the right on Road 117, or straight ahead on a single track. To continue the loop you'll go straight, but for now detour to the right on
Road 117 and follow it 0.6 mile to Midway Meadows. After enjoying
the meadows, return to the last junction and turn right on the Klickitat
Trail #7A. The trail now heads fairly steeply downhill. In 0.6 mile,
turn left on the Spring Creek Trail #115A. Follow it for 1.9 miles to
paved Road 5603. Turn right on the road and use it to cross over the
Muddy Fork, then pick up the Spring Creek Trail #115 on the left on
the opposite bank. In 0.4 mile the trail turns left and runs on dirt Road
042 for 0.3 mile, then continues 0.8 mile to the Keenes Trail #120A.
Turn left and follow it for 1.2 miles. Turn left on the High Lakes Trail
#116. In 0.2 mile, ford Spring Creek and immediately turn right on the
unsigned trail that will take you to Road 087 and return you to the
"new' campground loop at Keenes.

*Barb on
Riata,
Donna on
Zoey, and
Nancy on
Will,
cruising
along the
High Lakes
segment of
the loop.*

Pearly everlasting

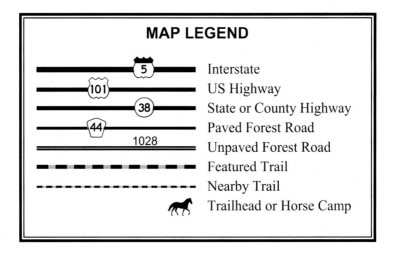

Lewis & Clark State Park

Washington State Parks

If you're traveling the I-5 corridor with your horse and you need a place to stop overnight, Lewis and Clark State Park is the spot for you. Located just 4 miles off the freeway, the park offers nice (and lightly used) overnight camping facilities on a first-come, first-served basis from May through September. Plus, the park offers 8 miles of equestrian trails that are a real delight. The trails run through an old-growth forest of Douglas-fir and red cedar and along wet prairies. The park

lies on a north-bound spur of the Oregon Trail, and the trees here are so big that when the pioneers came through, they had to build ramps over trees that had fallen across the route because they didn't have saws big enough to clear the trail.

Tex stands next to an old-growth cedar near the trail, providing perspective on the tree's size.

Getting to Lewis & Clark Park

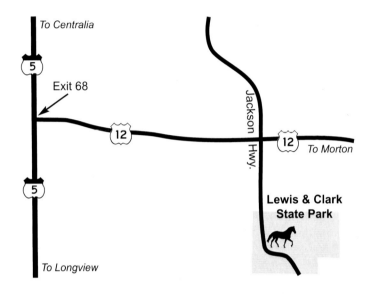

Tex enjoys her dinner at Lewis and Clark State Park.

Lewis & Clark Horse Camp

Directions: From I-5, take Exit 68 (Morton/Yakima Exit) and drive east on Hwy. 12. In 2.6 miles turn right on Jackson Hwy. and continue 1.6 miles to the park. About 500 feet past the park entrance, turn left at the sign for "Equestrian Trail and Group Camp 2." In 300 feet, turn left again at the sign for the Equestrian Area and enter the day-use parking area. Drive through the day-use area and turn right to reach the horse camp.

Elevation: 400 feet

Campsites: 5 equestrian sites. One large corral in site EQ2. All sites allow highlining or portable corrals. 3 sites are pull-throughs, 2 are back-in. All have fire pits and picnic tables.

Facilities: Manure bins in the horse camp. Porta-potty and potable water in the Community Center parking area 300 feet from the horse camp. The day-use area offers parking for 9 trailers, a manure bin, and garbage cans.

Permits: Camping fee; Discover Pass required for day use

Season: May 1 to September 30

Contact: Washington State Parks, 360-864-2643

Lewis & Clark Trails

Trail	Difficulty	Elevation	Round Trip
Lewis and Clark Horse Trails	Easy	400-600	5 miles

Lewis & Clark Park Horse Trails

Trailhead: Start at the equestrian area at Lewis & Clark State Park

Length: 8 miles round trip

Elevation: 400 to 600 feet

Difficulty: Easy

Footing: Suitable for barefoot horses. Trails can be very muddy after a rain, so please wait to ride until the trails dry out.

Season: May 1 - September 30

Permits: Discover Pass for day use; fee for overnight camping

Facilities: Manure bin and garbage can at the day-use area. Porta-potty and potable water at the adjacent Community Center parking area. No stock water on the trail.

Highlights: Eight miles of trail may not sound like a lot, but there is so much to delight the eye along these trails that it will seem like much

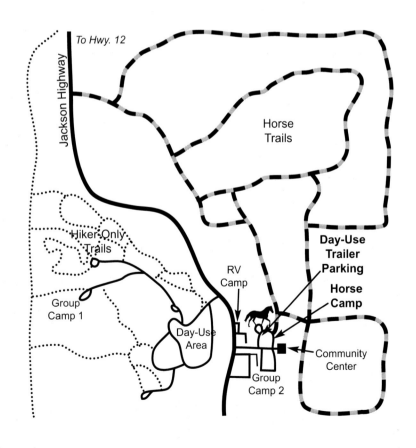

The northern trails run through old-growth forest.

more. The northern trails run through stunning old-growth forest, with giant cedars, Douglas-firs, and alders overhead, and vine maples, sword ferns, bracken, and blackberries beneath. The southern trails go along open wet-prairie meadows and through dense thickets, with seasonal wildflowers everywhere. The trails have excellent footing for trotting or gaiting, if you can bear to have the beautiful terrain go by that fast.

The Ride: From the day-use area, ride into the horse camp and pick up the trail between sites EQ3 and EQ4. Pick a direction, and go exploring!

The southern trails run beside open prairies.

Sword fern

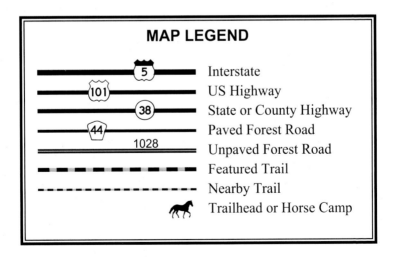

MAP LEGEND

🛡5	Interstate
101	US Highway
38	State or County Highway
44	Paved Forest Road
1028	Unpaved Forest Road
	Featured Trail
	Nearby Trail
🐎	Trailhead or Horse Camp

Long Beach

Long Beach, Washington

Long Beach, Washington boasts the longest beach in the world -- 26 miles from end to end. Horses are welcome on the entire length of the beach, except between Sid Snyder Ave. and Bolstad Drive from Memorial Day through September 15th. In addition to the fabulous beach riding, you can savor delicious seafood, charter a deep-sea fishing excursion, enjoy bumper cars and carnival games, or just take in the ocean views. You'll find several places you can stay with your horse along Long Beach, ranging from vacation homes with horse facilities to boarding barns that will permit you to stay overnight in your RV. And if you don't think your own horse can handle the excitement of being on the open beach, there are a couple of horse-rental outfitters that will provide horses and take you on guided rides.

Diana, Whitney, Debbie, Lydia, and Teresa ride Tommy, Dixie, Split, Magic, and Pops southward on Long Beach.

155

Getting to Long Beach

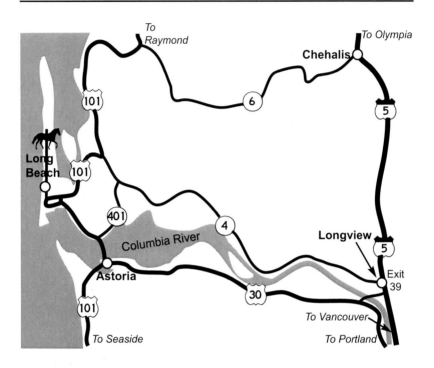

Long Beach Area Trails

Trail	Difficulty	Elevation	Round Trip
Long Beach	Easy	Sea Level	Varies

Long Beach Horse Facilities

Directions: From I-5, take Exit 39 (Longview/Kelso exit) and follow Hwy. 4 west for 61 miles. Turn left on Hwy. 101 and continue 15.5 miles, then turn right on Pacific Avenue in Long Beach.

Elevation: Sea level

Camping: Red Barn Arena 360-642-2009, redbarnarena.com
Peninsula Saddle Club, 360-642-2829, peninsulasaddle-club.com

Bed/Barns: Naytura Haus, 360-376-5312, nayturahaus.com
Sea Horse Acres, 503-954-2714, seahorseacres.com
Lake Lodge Bed & Barn, 360-665-3637, lakelodgebed-andbarn.com

Outfitters: Skippers Equestrian Center, 360-642-3676, www.skip-persequestrian.webs.com
Back Country Horse Rides, 360-642-2576

Season: Year round

Contact: Long Beach Peninsula Visitors Bureau, 360-642-2400

A beautiful sunny day on Long Beach.

Long Beach

Trailhead: The day-use parking areas at Long Beach that can best accommodate horse trailers are located at the west end of Bolstad Avenue, at the Seaview Beach Approach, and at Loomis Lake State Park

Length: Varies

Elevation: Sea level

Difficulty: Easy

Footing: Suitable for barefoot horses

Season: Year round

Permits: None

Facilities: Toilets at all trailheads, plus parking for several trailers. No stock water on the beach.

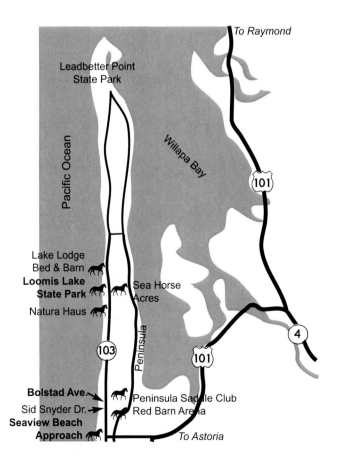

Highlights: Is there anything more exhilarating than cantering your horse down a hard-packed beach on a beautiful, sunny day?   You'll have plenty of opportunity to do this at Long Beach, where the white sand stretches before you for miles. In addition to traditional surfside activities like clamming, sand castle building, kite flying, and dog walking, Long Beach is open to vehicle traffic. Beach driving is a tradition here, so your horse will need to be able to cope with this trail "obstacle."

The Ride: The area between Sid Snyder Drive on the south and Bolstad Avenue on the north is closed to equestrian use from Memorial Day through September 15th. The nesting areas and trails at Leadbetter Point State Park are closed to horses. Otherwise, though, Long Beach enthusiastically welcomes horseback riders.

Diana, Teresa, and Lydia enjoy a ride on Tommy, Pops, and Magic.

Debbie canters Split down the beach.

Sand verbena

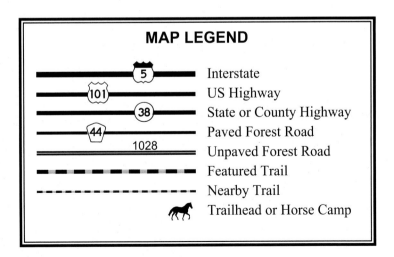

MAP LEGEND

⑤	Interstate
⑩⑪	US Highway
㊳	State or County Highway
㊹	Paved Forest Road
1028	Unpaved Forest Road
	Featured Trail
	Nearby Trail
🐎	Trailhead or Horse Camp

Mt. Adams Horse Camp

Gifford Pinchot National Forest

Mt. Adams Horse Camp and its nearby trails were built to provide low-elevation recreation opportunities for horseback riders. And what opportunities they are! With Mt. Adams visible from every campsite, this horse camp has arguably the best views of any in the Northwest. The campground has good amenities, with permanent highlines at each site and stock water in a trough. The nearby trails are a delight. You can ride a variety of short, easy loops near the camp, or you can venture farther afield and sample the higher-elevation trails. No matter what kind of trail riding you prefer, you'll find something at Mt. Adams to tickle your fancy, and plenty of trails to fill a long weekend.

Theresa and Breeze in the meadow
at Mt. Adams Horse Camp.

Getting to Mt. Adams Horse Camp

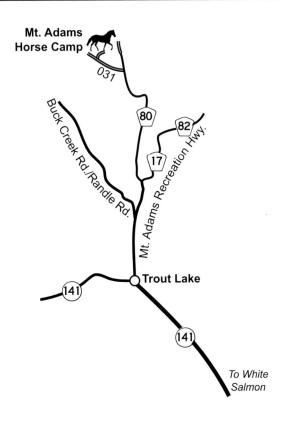

Mt. Adams Area Trails

Trail	Difficulty	Elevation	Round Trip
Big Tree Loop	Easy	2,700-3,200	5 miles
Buck/Morrison/Wicky Loop	Moderate	2,700-3,500	9.5 miles
Crofton Butte Loop	Challenging	2,700-4,750	17 miles
Snipes Mtn./Cold Spg. Loop	Challenging	3,500-6,200	13 miles
Unsigned Loop Trails	Easy	2,600-2,800	2.5-7 miles
White Salmon River Loop	Easy	2,200-2,700	5 miles

Mt. Adams Horse Camp

Directions: From Trout Lake, take the Mt. Adams Recreation Hwy. north. In 1.3 miles, stay to the right when Buck Creek Road/Randle Road goes off to the left. Continue 0.6 mile and turn left on Road 80, a paved 1-lane road. In 2.3 miles, turn left on gravel Road 031. The horse camp is on your right in 0.5 mile.

Elevation: 2,700 feet

Campsites: 12 sites, all with fire pits, picnic tables, and permanent highlines with cables. All sites but one are pull-throughs.

Facilities: Vault toilet, manure bins, stock water from a trough, accessible mounting ramp

Permits: Camping fee; no fee for day-use parking

Season: Early summer through fall

Contact: Mt. Adams Ranger District, 509-395-3400

Mt. Adams and high-lined horses at Mt. Adams Horse Camp.

Big Tree Loop

Trailhead: Start at Mt. Adams Horse Camp
Length: 5 miles round trip
Elevation: 2,700 to 3,200 feet
Difficulty: Easy
Footing: Hoof protection suggested
Season: Early summer through fall
Permits: Camping fee; no fee for day-use parking
Facilities: Toilet, potable water, and manure bins at the horse camp. No stock water on the trail.

Highlights: Volunteers from the Mt. Adams chapter of Back Country Horsemen created this fun loop that explores the forest north of the horse camp. The trail passes the impressive Trout Lake Big Tree -- at 202 feet tall and 84 inches in diameter, it is possibly the biggest pon-

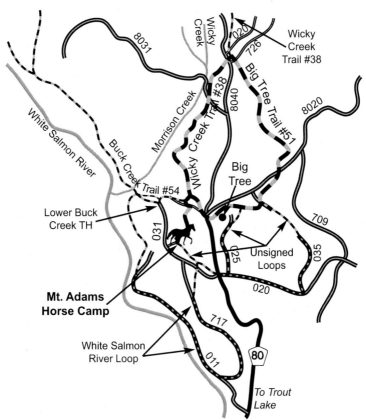

derosa pine on record. The trail loops east and then north, connecting with the Wicky Creek Trail #38 for the return leg of the loop. If you're willing to do a bit of exploring, more riding is possible on two unsigned trails nearby. (See the Unsigned Loop Trails pages in this chapter for more details.)

The Ride: Ride north across the meadow at Mt. Adams Horse Camp and veer left on the dirt road on the far side. In a short distance, turn right into the forest on a single-track trail. In 0.2 mile you'll reach a junction where the Buck Creek Trail #54 goes to the left. Go right instead, and in 200 feet you'll come to another junction where the Wicky Creek Trail #38 goes to the left. This will be your return route, so go to the right on the Big Tree Trail. In 0.5 mile you'll reach the very impressive Trout Lake Big Tree. Continue on the trail for another 2 miles, passing two unsigned trails that go off to the right. When you reach the junction with the Wicky Creek Trail #38, turn left and ride across Road 8040, picking up the trail on the other side and continuing 1.6 miles back to the junction of the Wicky Creek and Big Tree Trails. Jog to the right here for 200 feet, then turn left on the trail that will take you back to the horse camp.

Theresa on Breeze, Lydia on Magic, and Connie on Moose,
at the Trout Lake Big Tree.

Buck/Morrison/Wicky Loop

Trailhead: Start at Mt. Adams Horse Camp

Length: 9 miles round trip, or 9.5 miles round trip if you detour to the Wicky Creek Shelter

Elevation: 2,700 to 3,500 feet

Difficulty: Moderate

Footing: Hoof protection suggested

Season: Early summer through fall

Permits: Camping fee; no fee for day-use parking

Facilities: Toilet, potable water, and manure bins at the horse camp. Stock water is available on the trail.

Highlights: This loop provides a longer excursion than the short loops out of the horse camp. You'll ride on the Buck Creek Trail through a canyon deeply shaded by western redcedars and Douglas-firs, then climb a bit to reach the drier and more open forest along the Morrison Creek and Wicky Creek Trails. The Wicky Creek Shelter is definitely worth a detour.

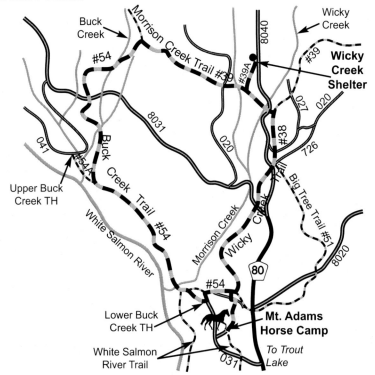

The Ride: Like most of the rides from Mt. Adams Horse Camp, this loop begins by heading north across the meadow, veering left on the dirt road at the edge of the meadow, then turning right on the single-track trail. At the junction 0.2 mile later, turn left on the Buck Creek Trail #54. In a little more than 0.3 mile you'll reach an unsigned trail junction. Either route will take you to the same spot, but the trail to the left is much more horse friendly, so veer left and soon you'll arrive at the Lower Buck Creek trailhead. Veer right to stay on the Buck Creek Trail, and in 0.2 mile the White Salmon River Trail comes in on the left. Stay right, and the trail will descend into a densely-forested canyon, where it crosses several bridges. In 1.5 miles, the spur trail to the Upper Buck Creek trailhead goes off to the left. Again stay right. The trail then climbs steadily for 2.1 miles to the junction with the Morrison Creek Trail #39. Turn right on it and continue 1.2 miles. At the junction with Trail #39A, turn left for a 0.3-mile detour to the Wicky Creek Shelter, a large wooden structure built as a haven for winter recreationists. It offers hitching rails and a picnic table, and is a good lunch spot. Return to the Morrison Creek Trail and turn left, and in 0.4 mile you'll reach Road 8040 and a good watering spot for your horses at Wicky Creek. Cross Road 8040 and turn right on the Wicky Creek Trail. Follow it for 2 miles, passing both junctions with the Big Tree Trail in the process. Just past the second Big Tree Trail junction, turn left to return to the horse camp.

Lydia, Theresa, and Connie ride Magic, Breeze, and Moose across a bridge on the Buck Creek Trail.

Crofton Butte Loop

Trailhead: Start at Mt. Adams Horse Camp
Length: 17 miles round trip
Elevation: 2,700 to 4,750 feet
Difficulty: Challenging
Footing: Hoof protection recommended
Season: Summer through fall
Permits: Camping fee; no fee for day-use parking
Facilities: Toilet, potable water, and manure bins at the horse camp. Stock water is available on the trail.

Highlights: This trail is long and has significant elevation change, and for half its distance it runs through the area burned by the 2012 Cascade Creek Fire. Some sections of the burned area have few living trees, but grass and wildflowers abound, and you now have some filtered views of Mt. Adams through the burned trees.

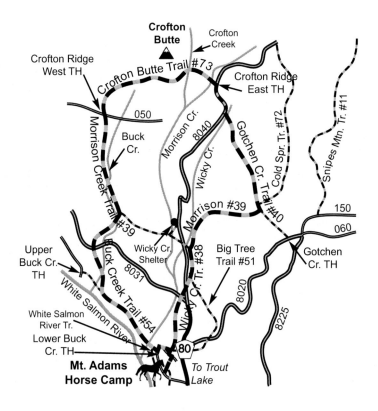

Connie rides Moose along the Crofton Butte Trail. The trees are all burned, but the bear grass is growing profusely.

The Ride: From Mt. Adams Horse Camp, head north across the meadow, veer left on the dirt road at the edge, then turn right on the trail into the forest. In 0.2 mile, turn left on Buck Creek Trail #54. About 0.2 mile after passing the Lower Buck Creek trailhead, the White Salmon River Trail comes in on the left. Stay right, and in another 1.5 miles the spur trail that leads to the Upper Buck Creek trailhead goes to the left. Ignore it and stay to the right, and in another 2.1 miles you'll come to the Morrison Creek Trail #39. Turn left on it and continue climbing steadily, and you'll cross Buck Creek in about a mile. After this you'll enter the area burned by the fire. About a mile later you'll reach the Crofton Ridge West trailhead. Pick up the Crofton Butte Trail #73. It continues uphill for about 0.5 mile, then veers right and levels out for 1.2 miles before traversing down the steep face of Crofton Butte and crossing Crofton and Morrison Creeks. At the Crofton Ridge East trailhead, turn right and ride down Road 8040 for 0.6 mile, then turn left on the Gotchen Creek Trail #40. Continue steadily downhill for 2 miles and stay to the right at the junction with the Cold Springs Trail #72. In 0.1 mile after that, turn right on the Morrison Creek Trail #39. After another 2.4 miles you'll reach the Wicky Creek Trail. You'll go straight ahead on it, but first take a detour to the right a short distance for a good watering spot next to Road 8040. Follow the Wicky Creek Trail 2.6 miles back to the horse camp, passing both junctions with the Big Tree Trail along the way.

Snipes Mtn./Cold Springs Loop

Trailhead: Start at the Snipes Mountain Trailhead or at Mt. Adams Horse Camp

Length: 13 miles round trip from Snipes Mountain Trailhead, or 24 miles round trip from Mt. Adams Horse Camp

Elevation: 3,550 to 6,200 feet from Snipes Mountain Trailhead, or 2,750 to 6,200 feet from Mt. Adams Horse Camp

Difficulty: Challenging

Footing: Hoof protection recommended

Season: Summer through fall

Permits: No fee to park at Snipes Mountain Trailhead

Facilities: Snipes Mountain Trailhead has parking for several trailers on the shoulder of a wide gravel road. There is stock water on the trail.

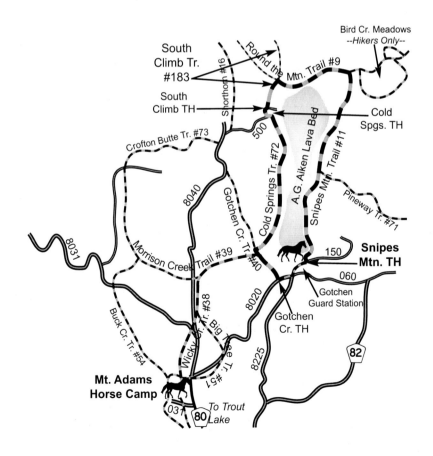

Highlights: This is a spectacular loop trail, with views of the A.G. Aiken Lava Bed, Mt. Adams, Mt. Hood, and beautiful bear grass in season.

Getting There: You can ride this trail from Mt. Adams Horse Camp by taking the Wicky Creek and Morrison Creek Trails to intersect with the Gotchen Creek Trail. However, we recommend trailering to the Snipes Mountain Trailhead. From Mt. Adams Horse Camp, drive Road 031 back to Road 80 and turn left. In 0.5 mile, turn right on Road 8020 and follow it 3.4 miles, then turn left on Road 150 and continue 0.7 mile to the trailhead.

The Ride: From the Snipes Mountain Trailhead, pick up the Snipes Mountain Trail #11 on the north side of Road 150. Follow it along the Aiken Lava Bed, and in 2 miles the Pineway Trail #71 will come in on the right. Continue straight, and after another 2.5 miles turn left on the Round the Mountain Trail #9. Ride 1.7 miles and turn left on the South Climb Trail #183. In 1.1 mile, it will take you to the South Climb Trailhead on Road 500. Ride down Road 500 for 0.2 mile to the Cold Springs Trailhead. Pick up the Cold Springs Trail #72 and ride it 3.4 miles, then turn left on the Gotchen Creek Trail #40 and take it 0.7 mile to Road 8020 and turn left. In 0.2 mile, turn left on Road 150 and continue along it to your trailer.

Jenny and Billie pause for a photo in front of Mt. Adams.
Photo courtesy of Jenny Webster.

Unsigned Loop Trails

Trailhead: Start at Mt. Adams Horse Camp

Length: 2.5 miles round trip for the short loop, 3.5 miles for the longer loop, and 7 miles if they are combined in a figure eight

Elevation: 2,600 to 2,800 feet

Difficulty: Easy, but the trails are unsigned so some navigation skills are required

Footing: Hoof protection suggested

Season: Early summer through fall

Permits: Camping fee; no fee for day-use parking

Facilities: Toilet, potable water, and manure bins at the horse camp. No stock water on the trail.

Highlights: These trails mostly follow old logging roads near the horse camp to create a couple of nice, short, forested loop routes. The trails aren't signed but they are well traveled, so if you want to do a bit

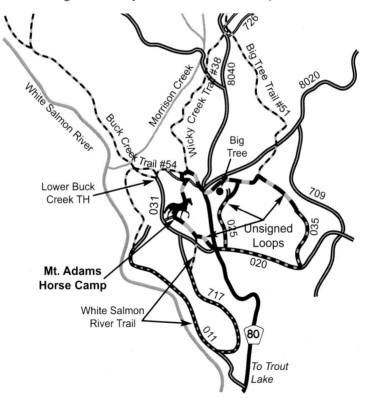

Lydia on Magic and Connie on Moose, cruising on the un-signed trails east of camp.

of exploring and have a good sense of direction (a GPS would be nice, too), you'll have no trouble finding and following them. If you repeat the segment that runs on Road 025 you can combine both loops into a 7-mile figure 8.

The Ride: Short Loop: Ride north across the meadow at Mt. Adams Horse camp and veer left on the dirt road on the far side. In a short distance, turn right into the forest on a single-track trail. In 0.2 mile the Buck Creek Trail #54 goes off to the left. Go right instead, and in 200 feet the Wicky Creek Trail #38 departs to the left. Veer right on the Big Tree Trail. After 0.5 mile you'll pass the Big Tree, and in another 0.1 mile an unsigned trail departs to the right. Turn right here and ride the unsigned trail (which soon runs on Road 025) for 0.7 mile to gravel Road 020. Turn right (or turn left here if you want to do the 7-mile figure eight) and continue to the stop sign at Road 80, then pick up the single-track trail across the road and to the right of the intersection. In 0.5 mile you'll reach the junction with the White Salmon River Trail. Turn right again, and in 0.2 mile you'll be back at the horse camp. Longer Loop: Follow the directions above, but instead of taking the first unsigned trail, go 0.2 mile farther and turn right on the second unsigned trail. Ride it 1.1 mile, then turn right on Road 020 and ride 0.6 mile to the stop sign at Road 80. Pick up the single-track trail across the road and follow it 0.5 mile, then turn right on the White Salmon River Trail and continue 0.2 mile back to the horse camp.

White Salmon River Loop

Trailhead: Start at Mt. Adams Horse Camp

Length: 5 miles round trip

Elevation: 2,200 to 2,700 feet

Difficulty: Easy

Footing: Hoof protection suggested

Season: Early summer through fall

Permits: Camping fee; no fee for day-use parking

Facilities: Toilet, potable water, and manure bins at the horse camp. No stock water on the trail.

Highlights: This delightful loop, created by volunteers from the Mt. Adams chapter of Back Country Horsemen, explores the area south of the horse camp. The trail runs steadily downhill and exits the national forest, then runs for a time along the rim (but not near the edge) of the

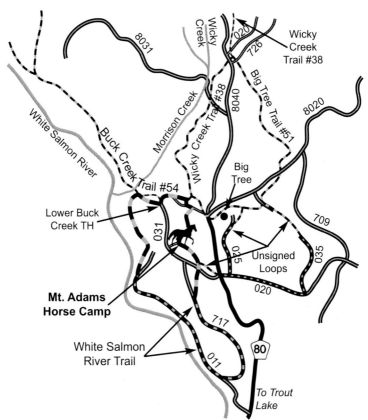

deep canyon carved by the White Salmon River. You'll hear the rushing of the water as the trail parallels the river. Then you'll head uphill to connect with the Buck Creek Trail #54 and circle back to camp.

The Ride: This trail doesn't depart by going north across the meadow. Instead, ride along the dirt road that rims the east side of the meadow and turn right on the single track trail you find there. In 0.2 mile, you'll cross Road 031, the road you drove on to reach the horse camp. The trail heads steadily downhill for 1.4 miles, coming out on dirt Road 011. Turn left and follow it for a little over 2 miles as it parallels the White Salmon River in the canyon far below you. The trail is well back from the edge of the canyon. When the trail intersects with the Buck Creek Trail #54, turn right and follow the Buck Creek Trail to the Lower Buck Creek Trailhead on Road 031. At the trailhead, turn left and almost immediately turn right to stay on the Buck Creek Trail. (Another trail goes straight ahead here, looping back to connect to the Buck Creek Trail near where you originally turned on to it, so avoid this trail.) Ride 0.4 mile and turn right on the trail that will take you back to the horse camp.

Lydia on Magic and Connie on Moose, riding along
the trail above the White Salmon River canyon.

Tree conks (tree-rot fungi) growing on
a Douglas-fir on the Wicky Creek Trail.

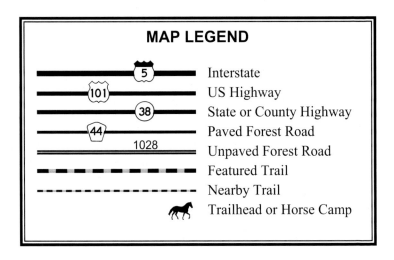

Pack Forest

University of Washington

Pack Forest, located a few miles south of Eatonville, is a research forest for the University of Washington's School of Forest Research. It was named for Charles L. Pack, who in the 1920s donated funds for the university to purchase forest land. The entire 4,300-acre forest is open for non-motorized recreational use and is popular with hikers, joggers, dog walkers, mountain bike riders, and equestrians. Gravel roads lace the area and offer good year-round riding. Single-track trails connect the forest roads to create numerous loop options, but the trails are muddy and slick when wet so are rideable only in summer and fall. The forest's highlights include three waterfalls on the Little Mashel River, and 1,740-foot Mt. Hugo, from the summit of which you can catch a view of the Olympic Range.

Middle Falls on the Little Mashel River at Pack Forest.

Getting to Pack Forest

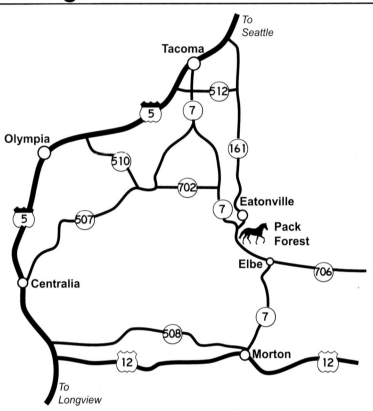

Pack Forest Trails

Trail	Difficulty	Elevation	Round Trip
Pack Forest Trails	Moderate	800-1,700	Varies

Pack Forest

Directions: From Eatonville, drive south on Hwy. 161 (Eatonville-La-Grande Road). Four miles after crossing the Mashel River, turn left on Hwy. 7. In 0.1 mile, turn left on an unsigned gravel road that leads to the gravel parking area for horse trailers.

Elevation: 800 feet

Campsites: No overnight camping permitted

Facilities: Parking for 4-8 trailers; no other facilities

Permits: None

Season: Year round

Contact: Pack Forest, 360-832-6534

The equestrian parking area at Pack Forest.

Pack Forest Trails

Trailhead: Start at the Pack Forest equestrian parking area

Length: Varies by route chosen

Elevation: 800 to 1,700 feet

Difficulty: Gravel roads are easy, single-track trails are moderate. A map will be very helpful in finding your way around.

Footing: Hoof protection recommended

Season: Year round for gravel roads, summer and fall for single-track trails

Permits: None

Facilities: Parking for 4-8 trailers. No stock water on the trail.

Highlights: Pack Forest offers delightful year-round riding in a pretty forest setting. You can ride to the three Little Mashel Falls (the falls are certainly not little, but the water flowing over them comes from the Little Mashel River), the largest of which is the Middle Falls, also

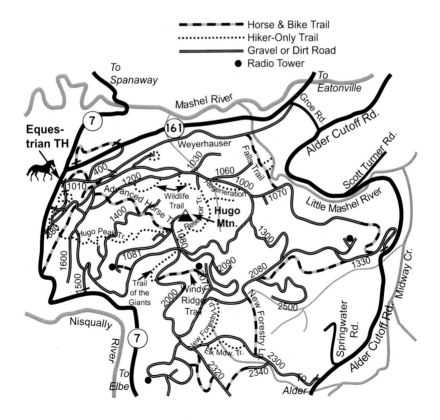

known as Bridal Veil Falls. You'll need to tie your horse and scramble down the steep hillside to get a view of the falls, but use care because the terrain can be treacherous when wet. Or you can ride to near the summit of Hugo Mountain, a 900-foot elevation gain that rewards you with views of the Olympics and the Nisqually River Valley. Or you can just explore the forest's network of roads and trails. No matter which way you go, Pack Forest will not disappoint.

The Ride: Ride around the large steel gate on the east side of the equestrian trailhead and pick up Road 1010. From here, you can explore the entire forest. Note that routes marked with yellow diamonds are open to hikers only, and routes marked with blue diamonds are open to equestrians and bikes as well as hikers. This is a working forest, so logging operations may temporarily close some sections of the forest. Dogs are allowed but must be under voice control, and hunting is allowed in season.

Tex heads out on one of the gravel roads at Pack Forest.

Ocean spray

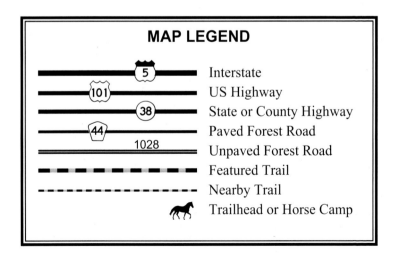

Packwood Lake

Gifford Pinchot National Forest

Some 12,000 years, ago a big chunk of Snyder Mountain broke off and slid into the valley below, damming up Lake Creek and creating the beautiful Packwood Lake. Since the Packwood Lake Trail runs through the Goat Rocks Wilderness to the lake, it's a bit of a surprise to arrive and see buildings on the lakeshore. It turns out the entire lake is outside the wilderness boundary. A hydro-electric plant has operated here since 1964, and there was once a small resort at the lake, complete with a general store and boat rentals. (The Forest Service shut down the resort in 1992 to protect this sensitive area.) Today Packwood Lake is a popular destination on its own, as well as a jumping-off spot for backpackers who want to explore the Goat Rocks Wilderness trails.

Agnes Island and Johnson Peak, seen across Packwood Lake.

Getting to Packwood Lake

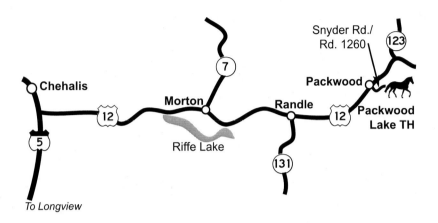

The historic Guard Station at Packwood Lake was used by forest rangers who patrolled the Goat Rocks Wilderness on horseback.

Packwood Lake Trailhead

Directions: From I-5, take Exit 68 (Yakima/White Pass) and head east on Hwy. 12 for 64.5 miles. Near the east end of Packwood, turn right on Snyder Road. In 0.7 mile, it becomes Road 1260. Follow it 4.9 miles to the paved day-use trailhead. Or, after 4.7 miles, turn left on Road 066 at a green gate and a sign for "Horse Trailer and ATV Trailer Parking Only" to reach a dirt parking area. Both parking areas have tight turnaround areas, so be sure to turn around when you arrive so you don't find yourself accidentally blocked in by other vehicles when it's time to leave. The dirt parking area doubles as a primitive camping site.

Elevation: 2,800 feet

Campsites: You can dispersed camp in the dirt parking area on Road 066, which has plenty of trees for highlining.

Facilities: Vault toilet and day-use parking for 3-5 trailers at the paved trailhead; parking for another 3-5 trailers but no water, toilet, or other facilities at the dirt trailer/ATV parking area below the paved trailhead

Permits: Northwest Forest Pass required

Season: Summer through fall

Contact: Cowlitz Valley Ranger District, 360-497-1100

Packwood Lake Area Trails

Trail	Difficulty	Elevation	Round Trip
Mosquito Lake	Challenging	2,750-4,800	13.5 miles
Packwood Lake Loop	Moderate	2,750-3,300	8-12.5 miles

Mosquito Lake

Trailhead: Start at the Packwood Lake trailhead

Length: 13.5 miles round trip

Elevation: 2,750 to 4,800 feet

Difficulty: Challenging

Footing: Hoof protection recommended

Season: Summer through fall

Permits: Northwest Forest Pass required

Facilities: Toilet and parking for 3-5 trailers at the paved parking area, plus parking for another 3-5 trailers at the dirt parking area off Road 066 just below the paved lot. Stock water is available on the trail.

Highlights: After you've ridden the delightful trail to Packwood Lake, you may want to continue farther and explore a bit more of this end of the Goat Rocks Wilderness. Mosquito Lake, located about 2 miles beyond the shore of Packwood Lake, would be a good choice. Be advised, however, that the trail to Mosquito Lake switchbacks steeply

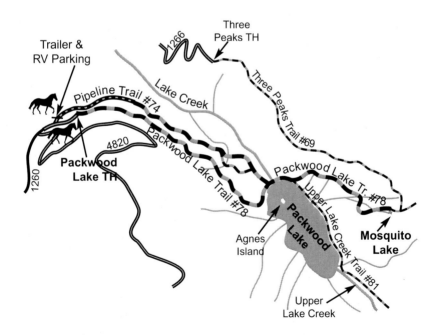

Karen rides Vaquera along the Packwood Lake Trail.

Karen and Vaquera on the Pipeline Trail.

up all the way to the lake and traverses some steep side slopes, so your horse will need to be in good condition. Tiny Mosquito Lake is aptly named. A campsite next to the lake makes a good lunch spot.

The Ride: Follow either the Packwood Lake Trail #78 or the Pipeline Trail #74 to Packwood Lake. (See the Packwood Lake Loop pages in this chapter for more details.) Continue over the Lake Creek bridge and along the shore of the lake for 0.5 mile to the junction with the Upper Lake Creek Trail #81. Veer left up the hill to stay on the Packwood Lake Trail. The trail switchbacks up 2,000 feet in 2 miles to reach tiny Mosquito Lake. It's a strenuous climb, so when you reach the lake both you and your horse will enjoy a break at this scenic spot.

Packwood Lake Loop

Trailhead: Start at Packwood Lake trailhead
Length: 8 miles round trip to the lake, or 12.5 miles round trip if you ride to the south end of the lake
Elevation: 2,750 to 3,300 feet
Difficulty: Moderate
Footing: Hoof protection recommended
Season: Summer through fall
Permits: Northwest Forest Pass required
Facilities: Toilet and parking for 3-5 trailers at the paved parking area, plus parking for another 3-5 trailers at the dirt parking area off Road 066 just below the paved lot. Stock water is available on the trail.

Highlights: It's a relatively easy jaunt through beautiful forest to pretty Packwood Lake, and you can make it into a loop by riding the Packwood Lake Trail #78 to and the Pipeline Trail #74 from the lake shore. In addition to a hydro-electric facility and a Forest Service building, the north end of the lake is home to the 1910-vintage Packwood Lake Guard Station, now undergoing restoration. From the bridge over Lake Creek you'll have a gorgeous view of Agnes Island

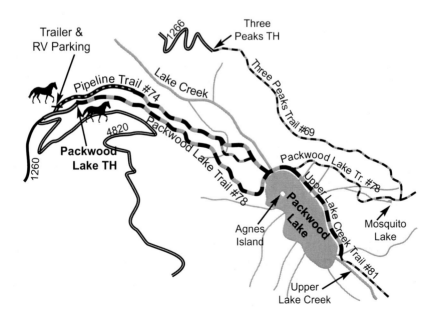

and Johnson Peak across the lake. If desired, you can continue along the eastern edge of the lake via the Upper Lake Creek Trail #81, which will take you past nice views of the lake and many primitive camp-sites to a good horse-watering spot at the south end of the lake.

The Ride: Begin on the Packwood Lake Trail #78, which departs from the east end of the paved parking area at the end of Road 1260. If you are parked in the dirt trailer parking area on Road 066 you'll need to ride up Road 1260 for 0.2 mile to reach the paved trailhead parking area. There's a view of Mt. Rainier from the paved trailhead, and after you've traveled about 0.8 mile along the trail you'll catch another view of the peak across an old clear-cut. Otherwise, though, this single-track trail runs entirely through the forest as it gains and then loses 500 feet of elevation and traverses a few fairly steep side hills.   The Pipeline Trail intersects with the Packwood Lake Trail on the shore of Packwood Lake just before the bridge over Lake Creek. Like the Packwood Lake Trail, the Pipeline Trail runs through the for-est, but it only experiences 150 feet of elevation change as it runs along a wide ATV track and then along a rocky gravel road. It offers views of the nearby ridges and the snow-covered peaks of the Tatoosh Wilderness to the north. The Pipeline Trail runs outside the wilderness boundary so it is shared with mountain bikes and ATVs. It ends at the dirt trailer parking area off Road 066.

Karen and Vaquera on the Upper Lake Creek Trail,
on the shore of Packwood Lake.

Canadian dogwood (fall)

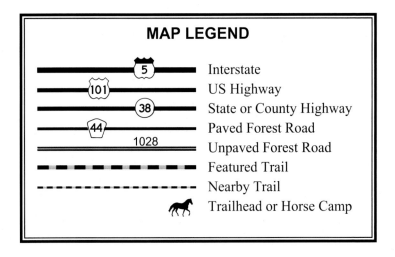

Peterman Hill

Cowlitz Wildlife Area, WA Dept. of Fish & Wildlife

Peterman Hill (sometimes called Peterman Ridge) is a 6,855-acre unit of the Cowlitz Wildlife Area. In addition to providing protected habitat for pileated woodpeckers, black-tailed deer, and Douglas squirrels, this area is home to black bears, cougars, elk, grouse, turkeys, beavers, and several types of amphibians. Peterman Hill features about 10 miles of trails that connect with forest roads to create a very nice trail network. The trails are open to hikers and mountain bikes as well as horses. Peterman Hill is a popular spot for fall hunting, so you might want to ride elsewhere during hunting season. Keep an eye out for logging trucks, as logging may occur here year-round.

*The trails at Peterman Hill go
through pretty second-growth forest.*

Getting to Peterman Hill

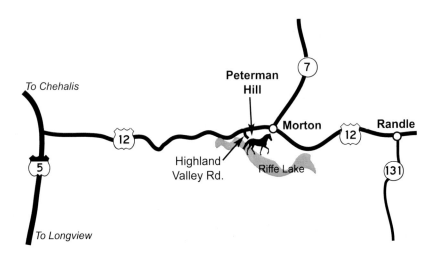

The large parking area can accommodate 10 or more trailers.

Peterman Hill

Directions: From I-5, take Exit 68 (Yakima/White Pass) and head east on Hwy. 12 toward Morton. In 27.5 miles, just before milepost 94, turn right on Highland Valley Road. In 100 yards veer right on Peterman Hill Road. Drive 0.9 mile to reach the large trailer parking area at the end of the county road, just past the car parking area.

Elevation: 1,550 feet

Campsites: Overnight camping is not permitted

Facilities: Vault toilet, hitching rails, garbage cans, parking for 10+ trailers

Permits: None

Season: Year round

Contact: Washington Dept. of Fish & Wildlife, (360) 496-6223

Peterman Hill Trails

Trail	Difficulty	Elevation	Round Trip
Peterman Hill Trails	Moderate	1,550-2,450	Varies

Peterman Hill Trails

Trailhead: Start at the Peterman Hill Trailhead

Length: Varies by route taken

Elevation: 1,550 to 2,450 feet

Difficulty: Moderate

Footing: Hoof protection recommended for the gravel forest roads

Season: Year round, though the single-track trails may be slippery after rain

Permits: Discover Pass required

Facilities: Toilet, hitching rails, garbage cans, parking for 10+ trailers. No stock water on the trail.

Highlights: The Peterman Hill section of the Cowlitz Wildlife Area offers a pleasant network of trails that explore several hills between

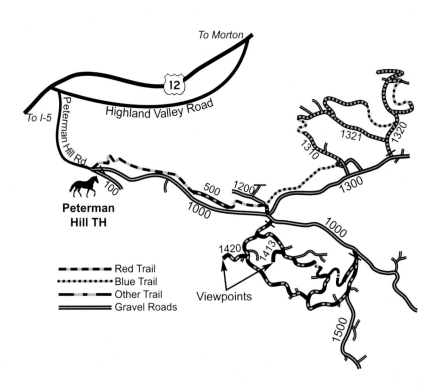

Hwy. 12 and Riffe Lake just west of Morton. The trails are sometimes single-track, and at other times they run along old closed logging roads. Open gravel logging roads also criss-cross the area, and you can combine them with the trails to create loops. The trails are open all year for horses, hikers, and mountain bikes.

The Ride: Pick up the trail on the north side of the trailer parking area, near the hitching rail. This is the Red Trail, which will take you up along the ridge above and roughly parallel to Road 1000. In a little over two miles, the trail crosses gravel Road 1200. Once you cross it you'll be on the Blue Trail (as indicated by the color on the signposts). The Blue Trail continues to the north and east, taking you to the highest elevations on Peterman Hill. Alternatively, when you reach Road 1200 you can turn right on it, ride across Road 1000, and explore additional trails that lie at the south end of the Peterman Hill area. These southern trails offer occasional views of the surrounding terrain.

Donna on Zoey, Barb on Riata, and Nancy on Will,
taking a break on the Blue Trail at Peterman Hill.

Goldenrod

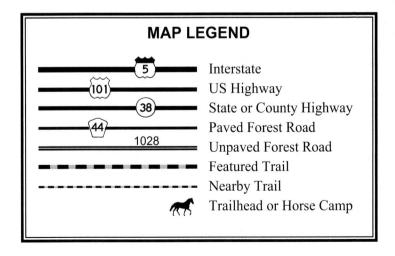

MAP LEGEND

Interstate
US Highway
State or County Highway
Paved Forest Road
1028 Unpaved Forest Road
Featured Trail
Nearby Trail
Trailhead or Horse Camp

Placid Lake

Gifford Pinchot National Forest

The Indian Heaven Wilderness is a fabulous place to experience on horseback. While you can access the popular south end of the Wilderness from the horse camp at Falls Creek (see the Falls Creek Horse Camp chapter), you can access the lesser-used north end by roughing it a bit at Placid Lake. There isn't a designated horse camp here, but you can dispersed camp at the Placid Lake Trailhead or, if you have a large group, at the nearby Lone Butte quarry. The terrain is horse friendly, the trails are phenomenal, and the forest, meadows, and lakes are breathtaking. So load up your hay and stock water, bring a shovel and toilet paper (sorry, no toilets here), and go!! Mosquitoes can be a problem in early to mid-summer, so the best time to go is August thru October.

Sawtooth Mountain provides a backdrop for the Surprise Lakes, just north of the Indian Heaven Wilderness.

Getting to Placid Lake

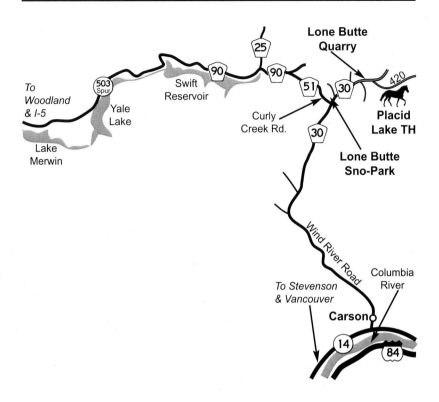

Placid Lake Trails

Trail	Difficulty	Elevation	Round Trip
Chenamus Lake	Moderate	4,100-4,300	3.5 miles
Deer, Bear, and Elk Lakes	Moderate	4,100-5,000	8 miles
Junction Lake Loop	Moderate	4,100-5,000	13 miles
Surprise Lakes	Moderate	4,100-5,100	16 miles
Wood Lake	Moderate	4,100-5,100	9.5 miles

Placid Lake Horse Camping

Directions: From Woodland, take Exit 21 from I-5 and go east on Hwy. 503/Lewis River Road toward Cougar. In 23 miles, Hwy. 503 goes to the right. Go straight on Hwy. 503-Spur, which becomes Road 90. In 23.7 miles, at the junction with Road 25, veer right on Road 90 toward Carson. Continue 4 miles and turn right on Road 51 (Curly Creek Rd.) In 5.1 miles, turn left on Road 30 (Wind River Road). In 1 mile, you'll see Lone Butte Sno-Park on the left.

From Stevenson, take Hwy. 14 east for 3.2 miles. Between mileposts 47 and 48, turn left on Wind River Road toward Carson. Drive 14.3 miles and veer right to stay on Wind River Road, which becomes Road 30. In 13.2 miles, Road 51 (Curly Creek Road) comes in on the left. After another mile (between mileposts 30 and 31) you'll see Lone Butte Sno-Park on the left.

All: At Lone Butte Sno-Park, veer right to stay on Road 30 (which turns to gravel) for 2.3 miles, then turn right again on Road 420. The Placid Lake Trailhead is on the right in 1.3 mile.

The Lone Butte quarry is a wide gravel area on the left side of Road 30, about 500 feet before you reach Road 420.

Elevation: 4,100 feet at Placid Lake trailhead

Campsites: Primitive camping only. If your party is small (2-3 trailers) you can camp at the Placid Lake Trailhead. If your party is large (up to 12 trailers), your best bet is to camp at the Lone Butte quarry.

Facilities: No toilet, no water at either Placid Lake Trailhead or Lone Butte Quarry. Plenty of trees for highlining at both spots.

Permits: None

Season: Summer through fall

Contact: Mt. Adams Ranger District, 509-395-3400

Photos of the Placid Lake Area

Johnny and Dolly relax on their highline on the edge of the Lone Butte quarry.

Peter and Gudrun ride Opie and Early along the shore of Chenamus Lake.

Lemei Lake

Delcie on China, Theresa on Breeze, Judy on Nine, Peter on Opie, Dave on Dolly, and Babs on Johnny, in a meadow near the Surprise Lakes.

Clear Lake

The horses enjoy a mid-morning snack in a meadow near Bird Mountain.

Chenamus Lake

Trailhead: Start at the Placid Lake Trailhead or the Lone Butte quarry

Length: 3.5 miles round trip from Placid Lake Trailhead, or 6 miles round trip from the Lone Butte quarry

Elevation: 4,100 to 4,300 feet from Placid Lake Trailhead, or 3,800 to 4,300 feet from the Lone Butte quarry

Difficulty: Moderate

Footing: Hoof protection suggested

Season: Summer through fall

Permits: None

Facilities: Parking for 2-3 trailers at Placid Lake Trailhead, depending on where hiker cars are parked. Parking for 10-12 trailers at the Lone Butte quarry. No facilities. Stock water is available on the trail.

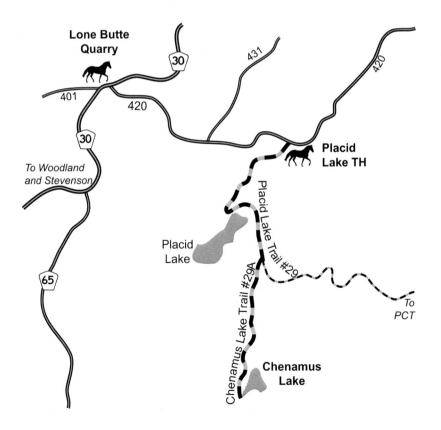

Delcie on China, Theresa on Breeze, and Judy on Nine, coming out of Chenamus Lake after the horses enjoy a refreshing drink.

Highlights: This is a short, easy jaunt from the trailhead, past pretty Placid Lake and on to shallow 4-acre Chenamus Lake, named for a mid-1800s Clatsop Indian chief. If you are staying for several days, the trail to Chenamus Lake is a nice warm-up ride for the day you arrive, or a pleasant wind-down ride for the day you depart. Along the trail, Douglas-firs, hemlocks, noble firs, and silver firs create a shady canopy, and huckleberries and bear grass dominate the understory.

The Ride: Start at the Placid Lake Trailhead on the south side of Road 420. Follow the Placid Lake Trail #29 for 0.6 mile to reach Placid Lake. Continue along the Placid Lake Trail, and soon you'll see the unsigned remains of the old Chenamus Lake Trail, now re-routed, going off to the right. Stay to the left on the Placid Lake Trail. In 0.6 mile you'll reach a signed junction with the new Chenamus Lake Trail #29A. Turn right here, and in 0.5 mile you'll reach Chenamus Lake. Retrace your steps to return to the trailhead.

Deer, Bear, and Elk Lakes

Trailhead: Start at the Placid Lake Trailhead or the Lone Butte quarry

Length: 8 miles round trip from Placid Lake Trailhead, or 10.5 miles round trip from the Lone Butte quarry

Elevation: 4,100 to 5,000 feet from Placid Lake Trailhead, or 3,800 to 5,000 feet from the Lone Butte quarry

Difficulty: Moderate

Footing: Hoof protection suggested

Season: Summer through fall

Permits: None

Facilities: Parking for 2-3 trailers at Placid Lake Trailhead, depending on where hiker cars are parked. Parking for 10-12 trailers at the Lone Butte quarry. No facilities. Stock water is available on the trail.

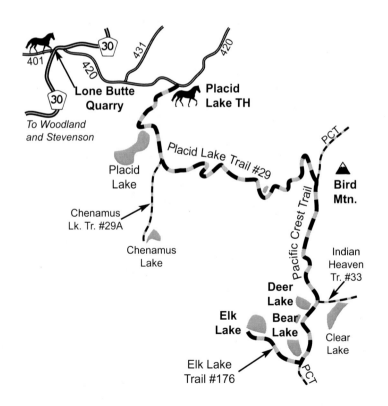

Highlights: This delightful out-and-back ride takes you past Placid Lake and along the PCT past a series of small, pretty meadows. The trail runs along a hillside high above Deer Lake, so all you can do is gaze down at it. However, you can ride to both Bear and Elk Lakes, and you'll find good spots along the shores of both lakes to water your horses and enjoy a leisurely lunch.

The Ride: Pick up the Placid Lake Trail #29 at the trailhead on the south side of Road 420. In 0.6 mile you'll reach Placid Lake. Just beyond the lake, stay to the left where the previous (now re-routed) Chenamus Lake Trail goes to the right. In another 0.6 mile you'll pass the junction with the new Chenamus Lake Trail #29A. Again stay to the left, and for the next 1.9 miles the trail will head steadily uphill to the PCT, passing several small meadows and a small unnamed lake along the way. Turn right on the PCT and follow it for 1.1 miles. At the junction with the Indian Heaven Trail #33, stay to the right on the PCT. In another 0.1 mile you'll see Deer Lake below you. Continue 0.2 mile and turn right on the Elk Lake Trail #176. It runs past Bear Lake and ends at Elk Lake in 0.6 mile.

Judy snaps a photo at Bear Lake. Because of its varying depths, the lake ranges from light aqua to deep sapphire blue.

Junction Lake Loop

Trailhead: Start at the Placid Lake Trailhead or the Lone Butte quarry

Length: 13 miles round trip from Placid Lake Trailhead, or 15.5 miles round trip from the Lone Butte quarry

Elevation: 4,100 to 5,000 feet from Placid Lake Trailhead, or 3,800 to 5,000 feet from the Lone Butte quarry

Difficulty: Moderate

Footing: Hoof protection suggested

Season: Summer through fall

Permits: None

Facilities: Parking for 2-3 trailers at Placid Lake Trailhead, depending on where hiker cars are parked. Parking for 10-12 trailers at the Lone Butte quarry. No facilities. Stock water is available on the trail.

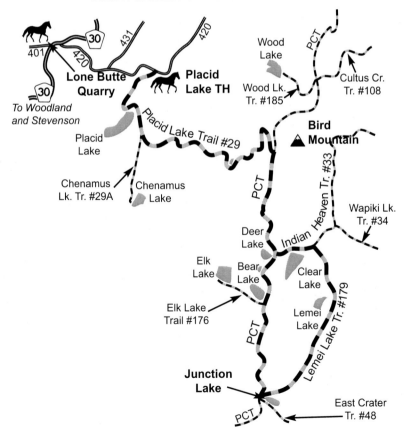

*Judy, Delcie, and Theresa ride Nine, China, and Breeze
along the shore of Junction Lake.*

Highlights: All by itself, Junction Lake would be a worthy destination for a trail ride. But this lollipop loop offers so much more. On the way out you'll enjoy a string of small meadows along the PCT and see Deer and Bear Lakes. At Junction Lake, you can picnic in lakeside meadows filled with huckleberries and bear grass. On the way home you'll have a nice view of Lemei Rock as you ride through the pretty meadows along the Lemei Lake Trail. Then you'll swing by beautiful Clear Lake before reconnecting with the PCT for your return journey.

The Ride: From the Placid Lake Trailhead, pick up the Placid Lake Trail #29 and follow it 3.1 miles to the PCT. Turn right on the PCT and continue 1.1 mile to the junction with the Indian Heaven Trail #33 and the sign pointing the way to Clear Lake. This will be your return route. For now, stay to the right on the PCT, passing Deer Lake and Bear Lake along the way. About a mile past the junction with the Elk Lake Trail you'll reach Junction Lake. Enjoy a leisurely lunch in the nearby meadows, then on the shore of Junction Lake turn left on the Lemei Lake Trail #179. Follow it 2.1 miles, past Lemei Lake and many meadows, and turn left on the Indian Heaven Trail #33. In the next 0.4 mile you'll pass Clear Lake and reach the PCT. Turn right here and retrace your steps back to the Placid Lake Trailhead.

Surprise Lakes

Trailhead: Start at the Placid Lake Trailhead or the Lone Butte quarry

Length: 16 miles round trip from Placid Lake Trailhead, or 18.5 miles round trip from the Lone Butte quarry

Elevation: 4,100 to 5,100 feet from Placid Lake Trailhead, or 3,800 to 5,100 feet from the Lone Butte quarry

Difficulty: Moderate

Footing: Hoof protection suggested

Season: Summer through fall

Permits: None

Facilities: Parking for 2-3 trailers at Placid Lake Trailhead, depending on where hiker cars are parked. Parking for 10-12 trailers at the Lone Butte quarry. No facilities. Stock water is available on the trail.

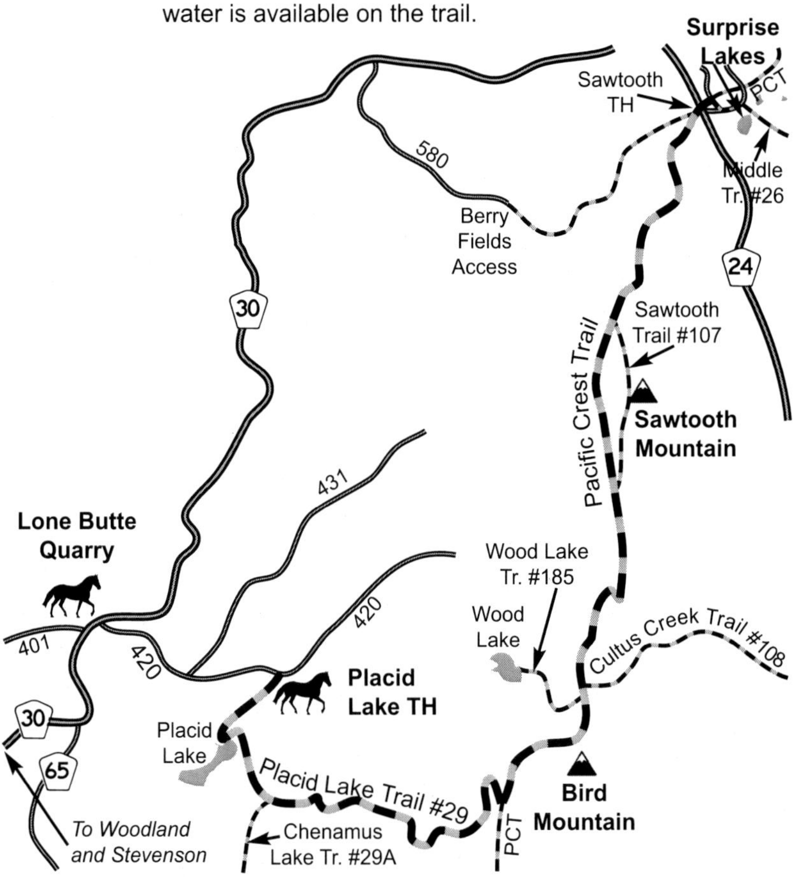

Highlights: The Surprise Lakes lie just outside the northern boundary of the Indian Heaven Wilderness. This out-and-back ride features dense forest, small meadows, several beautiful lakes, and a nice view of Mt. Adams.

The Ride: From Placid Lake Trailhead, pick up the Placid Lake Trail #29, and follow it 3.1 miles to the PCT. Turn left. The PCT runs along the flank of Bird Mountain for about 0.9 mile, then passes the junctions with the Wood Lake Trail #185 on the left and the Cultus Creek Trail #108 on the right. Stay on the PCT and after about 1.2 miles you'll ride along the base of Sawtooth Mountain, past two junctions with the Sawtooth Trail #107. About 1.4 miles after the second Sawtooth Trail junction you'll reach the Sawtooth Trailhead on gravel Road 24. (Just before the trailhead, check out the beautiful view of Mt. Adams from the top of the low hill on the right.) Cross Road 24 and continue on the PCT for a short distance, then veer right on a dirt road that will take you to the largest of the Surprise Lakes.

Dave, Babs, Judy, and Theresa on Dolly, Johnny, Nine, and Breeze, enjoying the view of Mt. Adams from the PCT near the Surprise Lakes.

Wood Lake

Trailhead: Start at the Placid Lake Trailhead or the Lone Butte quarry

Length: 9.5 miles round trip from Placid Lake Trailhead, or 12 miles round trip from the Lone Butte quarry

Elevation: 4,100 to 5,100 feet from Placid Lake Trailhead, or 3,800 to 5,100 feet from the Lone Butte quarry

Difficulty: Moderate

Footing: Hoof protection suggested

Season: Summer through fall

Permits: None

Facilities: Parking for 2-3 trailers at Placid Lake Trailhead, depending on where hiker cars are parked. Parking for 10-12 trailers at the Lone Butte quarry. No facilities. Stock water is available on the trail.

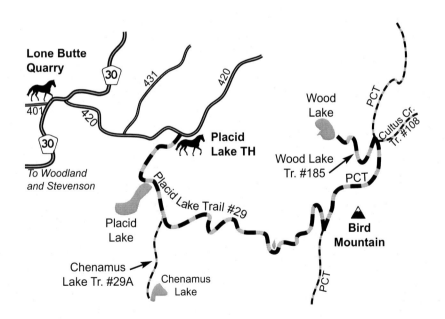

Dave on Dolly, Babs on Johnny, and Delcie on China, on the PCT near Wood Lake.

Highlights: The trail to Wood Lake is a delightful out-and-back ride that takes you through a dense forest of Douglas-fir, true fir, and hemlock. You'll ride past some small meadows dotted with huckleberries and bear grass and along a small lake that is so sheltered from the wind that it's hard to tell the crystal-clear reflections in the water from the real thing. You'll find a nice lunch spot on the shore of pretty Wood Lake.

The Ride: From the Placid Lake Trailhead, it's 0.6 mile on the Placid Lake Trail #29 to its namesake lake, then another 2.5 miles to the Pacific Crest Trail. Turn left on the PCT and ride along the lower flank of Bird Mountain. In 0.9 mile, you'll reach the junctions with the Cultus Creek Trail #108 (to the right) and the Wood Lake Trail #185 (to the left). Turn left on the Wood Lake Trail, and in 0.6 mile it will take you to the pleasant shore of Wood Lake.

Cauliflower mushroom, growing on the bark of a tree.

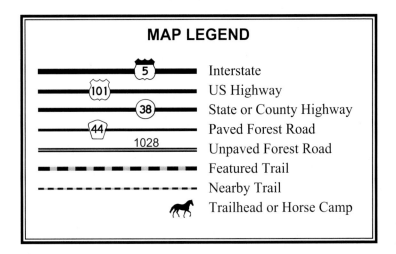

MAP LEGEND

══════ **⑤** ══════	Interstate
═══**⟨101⟩**═══	US Highway
══════ **㊳** ══════	State or County Highway
═══**⟨44⟩**═══	Paved Forest Road
════════ 1028 ════════	Unpaved Forest Road
▬ ▬ ▬ ▬ ▬ ▬	Featured Trail
- - - - - - - - - - - -	Nearby Trail
🐎	Trailhead or Horse Camp

Rock Creek Campground

Yacolt Burn State Forest, WA Dept. of Nat. Resources

In September 1902, the Yacolt Fire torched 238,900 acres (370 square miles) of forest in SW Washington, traveling 36 miles in 36 hours and killing 38 people. Fueled by dry conditions and driven by hard east winds, the fire buried Portland under a half inch of ash and became the largest forest fire in Washington history. Some of the area burned by the fire is now the Yacolt Burn State Forest. The only horse camp in the Forest is Rock Creek Campground, which provides access to splendid trails that explore the nearby hills. The trails run through working forestlands, alternating between shady forest, tree plantations, and clearcut areas with abundant wildflowers and panoramic views. The trails near Rock Creek are popular with mountain bike riders and sometimes have short lines of sight, so keep a watchful eye out. In the coming years, DNR is considering several new trails that will provide more loop opportunities for all users, as well as a bike-only trail that will hopefully reduce mountain bike traffic on some of the other trails.

Mt. St. Helens

Lydia and Magic gaze out at Mt. St. Helens across a clear cut on the Larch Mountain segment of the Tarbell Trail.

Getting to Rock Creek

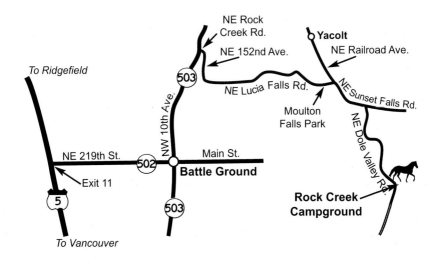

Diamond and Magic relax at Rock Creek Campground.

Rock Creek Campground

Directions: From 1-5, take Exit 11 and head east on Hwy. 502/NE 219th St. toward Battle Ground. In 6 miles turn left on Hwy. 503/NW 10th Ave. Continue 5.6 miles and turn right on NE Rock Creek Rd. In 0.3 mile the road name changes to NE 152nd Ave. In another 1.2 miles the road veers left and becomes NE Lucia Falls Rd. About 8.2 miles after turning off Hwy. 503 you'll pass Moulton Falls Park. In 0.3 mile after that, turn right on NE Sunset Falls Rd. Continue 2.0 miles, then turn right on NE Dole Valley Rd. Drive another 5.0 miles and turn left into the campground. A tiny brown sign on the right indicates the entrance.

Elevation: 1,050 feet

Campsites: 19 sites, 13 of which permit equestrian use. Each site has a 2-horse corral (some in a 4-horse configuration and shared with an adjacent campsite), fire ring, and picnic table. Most sites are pull-throughs and several have room for 2 trailers.

Facilities: Vault toilets, manure bins, stock water troughs, camp host. Two small day-use parking areas, plus a group shelter with barbecue grills. Accessible mounting ramp.

Permits: Discover Pass required

Season: Year round

Contact: Washington Dept. of Natural Resources, 360-577-2025

Rock Creek Area Trails

Trail	Difficulty	Elevation	Round Trip
Bells Mountain Trail	Moderate	850-1,550	17.5 miles
Cedar Creek Falls	Moderate	1,050-1,400	6.5 miles
Hidden Falls	Moderate	1,050-2,550	17 miles
Larch Mountain	Moderate	1,050-3,400	13.5 miles
Tarbell Trailhead	Moderate	1,050-1,900	6.5 miles

Bells Mountain Trail

Trailhead: Start at Rock Creek Campground
Length: 17.5 miles round trip to the Mt. St. Helens viewpoint
Elevation: 850 to 1,550 feet to the Mt. St. Helens viewpoint
Difficulty: Moderate to the Mt. St. Helens viewpoint
Footing: Hoof protection recommended -- very rocky trail
Season: Spring through fall. Trails and bridges are slick when wet.
Permits: Discover Pass required for camping or day-use
Facilities: Toilet, stock water, manure bins, and day-use parking for 6-7 trailers at the horse camp. Stock water is available on the trail.

Highlights: This trail runs along pretty Cedar Creek and up onto Bells Mountain for a panoramic view of the Dole Valley, the nearby hills, and Mt. St. Helens. You can continue beyond the Mt. St. Helens viewpoint to Moulton Falls Park, but the trail from the viewpoint down to Moulton Falls Park is not horse friendly and we would avoid it.

The Ride: Pick up the Tarbell Trail next to the water trough and day-use parking area near the entrance to the "A" Loop at Rock Creek Campground, then follow the directions for the Cedar Creek Falls ride later in this chapter. From Cedar Creek Falls, continue along the creek on the Bells Mountain Trail for 2 miles to a nice watering spot. The

Mt. St. Helens

Lydia and Connie ride into a clearcut area with a view of Mt. St. Helens. On this day the top of the mountain was shrouded in clouds.

trail then leaves the creek and begins climbing Bells Mountain, running alternately through clear cut areas and open forest. It's another 5.5 miles (and an elevation gain of 1,250 feet) to reach a clear-cut area near the high point of the trail and a good view of Mt. St. Helens. The trail continues on to Moulton Falls Park, but beyond the viewpoint the trail is not horse friendly. It loses 1,100 feet of elevation in 1.5 miles, running down a very steep side hill that was recently clear cut. On this stretch of trail the edge of the trail is very loose, the trail is covered with pebbles that roll under your feet like marbles, and the drop-off is several hundred feet. So after you enjoy the view of Mt. St. Helens, retrace your step to Rock Creek Campground.

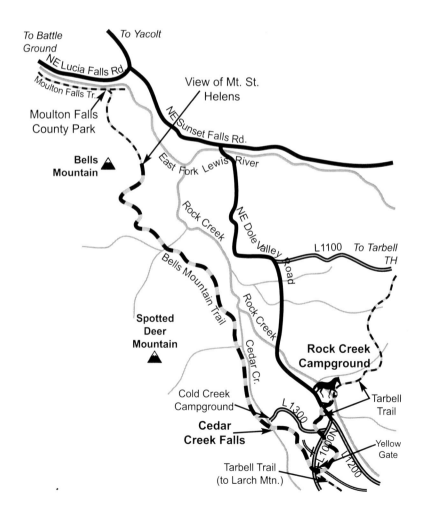

Cedar Creek Falls

Trailhead: Start at Rock Creek Campground

Length: 6.5 miles round trip

Elevation: 1,050 to 1,400 feet

Difficulty: Moderate

Footing: Hoof protection recommended

Season: Spring through fall. Trails and bridges are slick when wet.

Permits: Discover Pass required for camping or day-use

Facilities: Toilet, stock water, manure bins, and day-use parking for 6-7 trailers at the horse camp. Stock water is available on the trail.

Highlights: Cedar Creek Falls is a small but pretty waterfall near the Cold Creek Campground. The first and last miles of this ride are beau-

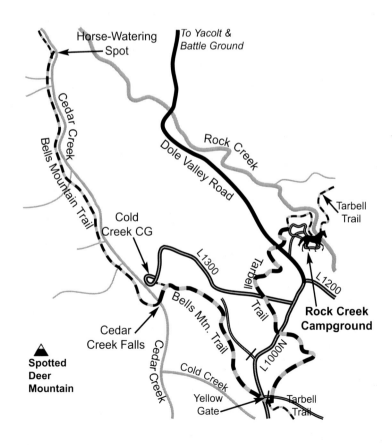

Cedar Creek Falls

tifully forested. In between, the trail runs through several plantations where the trees range from seedlings to 20 feet high. Abundant wild-flowers line the trail in season.

The Ride: Pick up the Tarbell Trail next to the water trough and day-use parking area near the entrance to the "A" Loop. The trail crosses Dole Valley Road and heads southward. In 1.8 miles you'll come to a gravel road just uphill from a yellow gate. Follow the trail across the gravel road and down toward the gate. Just before you reach the gate, turn right on a single-track trail that will take you across Road L1000N to the Bells Mountain Trail on the other side. Follow the Bells Mountain Trail for 1.2 miles to a junction. The trail to the right goes to Cold Creek Campground, and the trail to the left goes to Cedar Creek Falls. Go to the left, and in 0.1 mile you'll arrive at Cedar Creek Falls and the bridge over Cedar Creek. The best view of the falls is from the bridge.

Bonus Ride: If you haven't had enough riding when you reach Cedar Creek Falls, you can continue on the Bells Mountain Trail for another 2 miles as it runs along pretty Cedar Creek. You'll find an excellent horse watering spot at the point where the trail veers away from the creek and begins climbing Bells Mountain, so this is a good point to turn around and retrace your steps to the trailhead. This extended ride is 10.5 miles round trip, with very little elevation change.

Hidden Falls

Trailhead:	Start at Rock Creek Campground
Length:	17 miles round trip
Elevation:	1,050 to 2,550 feet
Difficulty:	Moderate
Footing:	Hoof protection recommended
Season:	Early summer through fall. Trails and bridges are slick when wet.
Permits:	Discover Pass required for camping or day-use
Facilities:	Toilet, stock water, manure bins, and day-use parking for 6-7 trailers at the campground. Stock water is available on the trail.

Highlights: Easily the most scenic spot on the entire Tarbell Trail, Hidden Falls is a gem. Coyote Creek drops 92 feet over a rock ledge into a pool next to the trail bridge over the creek. Beautiful! DNR and equestrian volunteers are working on a new trail from Rock Creek

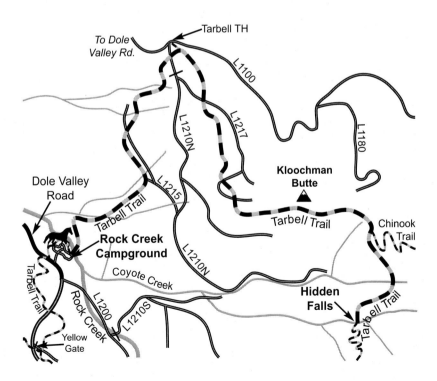

Hidden Falls

Campground to Hidden Falls, which will shorten the distance to the falls and add a loop option to this ride. Stay tuned!

The Ride: Pick up the Tarbell Trail at the day-use parking area on the campground's B Loop. In 100 yards you'll cross a bridge over Rock Creek. The trail goes steadily uphill for 3 miles to the junction with the spur trail that leads to the Tarbell Trailhead. Keep right at this junction. For 2 more miles the trail continues uphill as it heads toward Kloochman Butte, with a total elevation gain of 1,500 feet over 5 miles. The trail then levels out for the remaining 3 miles to Hidden Falls. About 1.5 miles after the trail stops gaining elevation, the Chinook Trail goes off to the left. Stay right, and in another 0.8 mile you'll reach a stream crossing where you can water your thirsty, hardworking horse. About 0.9 mile after that you'll reach the lovely Hidden Falls. Retrace your steps to return to Rock Creek Campground.

Larch Mountain

Trailhead: Start at Rock Creek Campground

Length: 13.5 miles round trip

Elevation: 1,050 to 3,400 feet

Difficulty: Moderate

Footing: Rocky trail -- hoof protection recommended

Season: Early summer through fall. Trails and bridges are slick when wet.

Permits: Discover Pass required for camping or day-use

Facilities: Toilet, stock water, manure bins, and day-use parking for 6-7 trailers at the campground. Stock water is available on the trail.

Highlights: This trail goes from Rock Creek Campground to near the top of Larch Mountain. The trail gains significant elevation as it alternates between green, shady forest and exposed clear-cut hillsides with abundant wildflowers in season. Popular with mountain bikes,

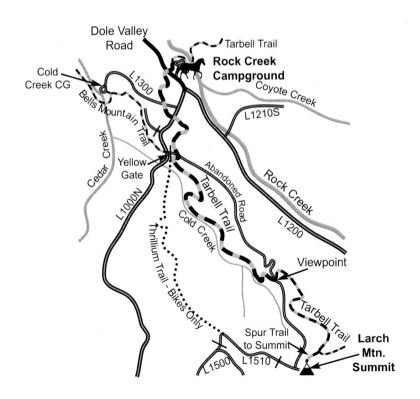

this segment of the Tarbell Trail has limited lines of sight in some places, so keep a sharp eye out for fellow trail users.

The Ride: Pick up the Tarbell Trail next to the water trough and day-use parking area near the entrance to the "A" Loop. The trail crosses Dole Valley Road and heads southward. In 1.8 miles the trail crosses a gravel road just uphill from a yellow gate. Follow the trail across the gravel road and down toward the gate. Just before you reach the gate you'll come to a junction with a single-track trail. Turn left on it to continue on the Tarbell Trail. It runs steadily uphill for about 3 miles to an abandoned gravel logging road that runs through a clearcut with a nice view of Larch Mountain. If you turn around at this point, you'll end up riding a 10-mile round trip with an elevation gain of 1,300 feet. Or you can continue another 1.8 miles to the summit, with an additional elevation gain of 1,000 feet. To reach the summit, after 1.5 miles you'll turn right on a spur trail that leaves the Tarbell Trail and climbs 0.3 mile to the top. The views are panoramic.

Lydia rides Magic along the Tarbell Trail toward Larch Mountain.

Tarbell Trail to Tarbell Trailhead

Trailhead: Start at Rock Creek Campground

Length: 6.5 miles round trip

Elevation: 1,050 to 1,900 feet

Difficulty: Moderate

Footing: Hoof protection suggested

Season: Early summer through fall. Trails and bridges are slick when wet.

Permits: Discover Pass required for camping or day-use

Facilities: Toilet, stock water, manure bins, and day-use parking for 6-7 trailers at the horse camp. No stock water on the trail.

Highlights: The Tarbell Trail is named for George Lee Tarbell, a recluse who lived in the area in the early 1900s. His shack was acces-

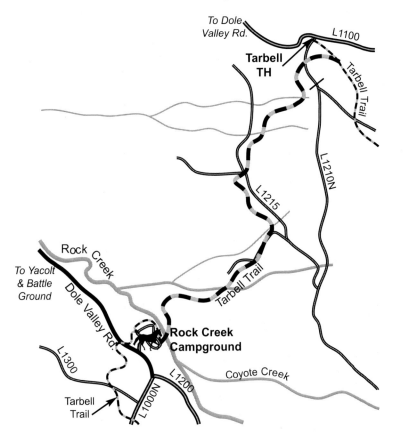

sible only by a foot trail that the current trail roughly follows. The 25-mile Tarbell Trail connects to the Bells Mountain Trail and is part of the Chinook Trail, which will eventually be a 300+ mile trail that circles the Columbia River from Vancouver to Maryhill. From Rock Creek Campground it's a fun ride to the top of the hill near the Tarbell Trailhead. The summit area has recently been logged so it offers some nice views.

The Ride: Pick up the Tarbell Trail at the day-use area on the campground's B Loop. In 100 yards you'll cross a bridge over Rock Creek. The trail heads steadily uphill for 3.2 miles, cresting the hill near the Tarbell Trailhead. Along the way you'll go through beautiful stretches of Douglas-fir forest, with alder, maple, vine maple, sword ferns, and bracken in the understory. The dense forest segments are interrupted by clearcut sections, with juvenile Douglas-fir trees growing among the stumps, slash piles, and wildflowers. Clearcuts may not be your favorite places to ride, but they do offer expansive views, open lines of sight so you can see bicyclists coming, and abundant wildflowers in season. When you reach the top of the hill, you can retrace your steps to return to Rock Creek Campground, or you can continue on the Tarbell Trail. See the pages in this chapter for the Hidden Falls ride for inspiration.

Theresa on Breeze and Lydia on Magic, riding into a clearcut filled with ferns, hawkweed, fireweed, and oxeye daisies.

Star Solomon's Seal

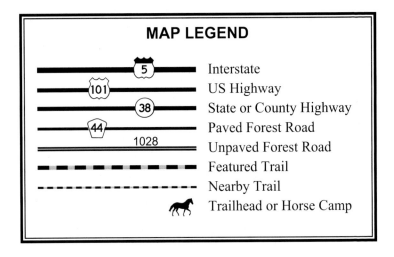

MAP LEGEND

Interstate

US Highway

State or County Highway

Paved Forest Road

Unpaved Forest Road

Featured Trail

Nearby Trail

Trailhead or Horse Camp

Sahara Creek Campground

Washington State Dept. of Natural Resources

Five miles east of the town of Elbe, Sahara Creek Campground provides access to the Nicholson Horse Trail System, a splendid 65-mile trail network that explores the Elbe Hills. The trails were created specifically for equestrian use, and mountain bikes are not allowed here. The Nicholson trails are horse friendly, with wide tread, no steep dropoffs, and well-signed junctions. Your horse will need to be in shape, though, because the trails gain significant elevation. The Elbe State Forest is a working forest, so in addition to experiencing beautiful stands of Douglas-fir, alders, and maples, you'll also ride through clear-cuts that offer panoramic views. The DNR website provides current information about any trails that may be temporarily closed for logging.

Stupendous views of Mt. Rainier await you on the trails in the Elbe Hills near Sahara Creek Campground.

227

Getting to Sahara Creek

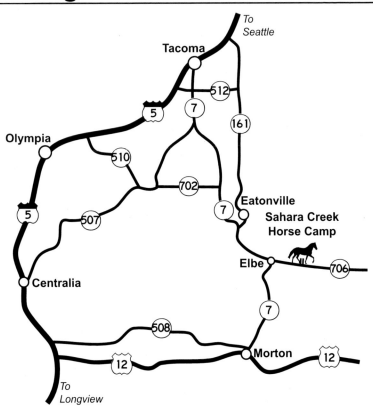

Nicholson Horse Trails

Trail	Difficulty	Elevation	Round Trip
Nicholson Horse Trails	Challenging	1,500-3,100	65 miles
ADA Loop	Easy	1,500-1,600	2.2 miles
Peanut Loop	Moderate	1,500-2,100	4.5 miles
Anvil Loop	Challenging	1,500-3,000	12.5 miles
Beaver Cr./Buck Crossing Lp.	Challenging	1,500-2,700	9.5 miles
Holly/Fawn Loop	Moderate	1,500-2,150	5.5 miles

Sahara Creek Campground

Directions: From Elbe, drive east on Hwy. 706 for 5 miles. Just 200 feet past milepost 5 and the large sign for the Mt. Tahoma Trails, turn left into the campground. The campground sign is very small and easy to miss.

Elevation: 1,500 feet

Campsites: 20+ large sites, with room for 40 trailers. Highline posts are placed every 30 feet around most of the perimeter of the campground. (Bring your own highline rope.) Some sites are back-in, others are pull-through, and all can accommodate more than one trailer. All sites have fire pits and picnic tables. Please haul your manure home or disperse it outside the camp boundaries.

Facilities: Vault toilet, potable water from a spigot. Day-use area has accessible mounting ramp, hitching rails, potable water spigot, picnic tables, and vault toilet. No manure bin.

Permits: Discover Pass required

Season: Summer through fall

Contact: South Puget Sound Region, Washington Dept. of Natural Resources, 360-825-1631

Sundance and Zoey relax on their highline at Sahara Creek.

Nicholson Horse Trails

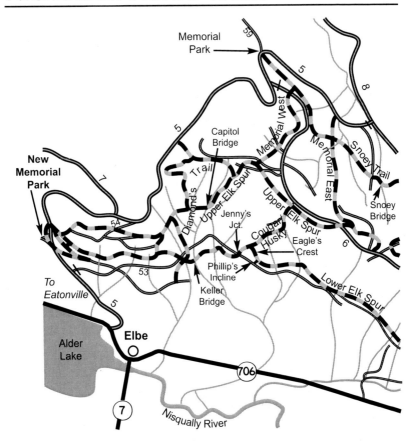

Highlights: This chapter focuses primarily on the trails in the Nicholson Horse Trails System that are easily accessible from Sahara Creek Campground. While there are many possible loops, the ones featured here were selected to provide a sampling of the terrain and distances you will encounter. Please go exploring--this is a wonderful place to ride.

In addition to Sahara Creek Horse Camp, you can access the Nicholson trails from the New Memorial Park trailhead on the west side and from Beaver Creek Camp on the northeast side. It is 8.4 miles from Sahara Creek Campground to New Memorial Park via the Lower Elk Spur Trail.

Note that hunting is permitted in Elbe State Forest in season. There is also a nearby shooting range, so if you hear gunfire when it isn't hunting season it is most likely coming from the shooting range.

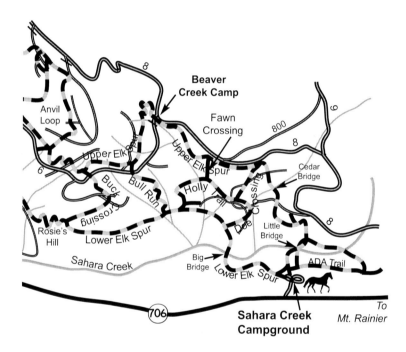

Getting To the Alternate Trailheads: To drive to the trailhead at New Memorial Park, go west out of Elbe on Hwy. 7 and turn north on Road 5. Follow it 2 miles to the trailhead. This is a very steep road, so 4-wheel drive is a must.

To drive to Beaver Creek Camp, take Hwy. 706 east from Elbe for 6.1 miles. Turn left on Stoner Road, which soon becomes Road 8. Follow Road 8 for 4.3 miles, then turn left on a spur road that will take you to the trailhead parking area in a short distance.

ADA Loop and Peanut Loop

Trailhead: Start at Sahara Creek Campground

Length: The ADA Loop is 2.2 miles round trip and the Peanut Loop is 4.5 miles round trip. Combine them both for a 5.2-mile ride.

Elevation: 1,500 to 1,600 feet for the ADA Loop, or 1,500 to 2,100 feet for the Peanut Loop

Difficulty: Easy for the ADA Loop, moderate for the Peanut Loop

Footing: Hoof protection suggested

Season: Summer through fall

Permits: Discover Pass required for day use or overnight camping

Facilities: Toilet, potable water, and ADA-accessible mounting ramp at the horse camp. No stock water on the trail.

Highlights: These two routes are the shortest loops in the Nicholson Horse Trails network. The ADA Loop is an easy jaunt through lush

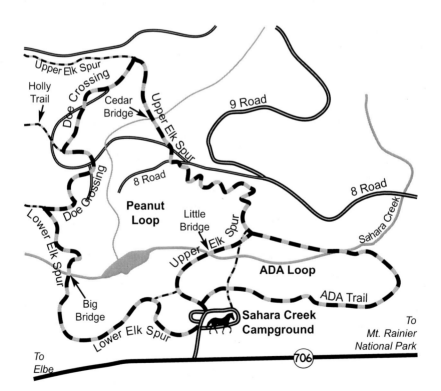

forest on fairly level ground. The Peanut Loop is only 4.5 miles round trip but it's quite a bit more challenging than the ADA Loop, crossing 3 bridges and gaining 600 feet of elevation in a mile, with short stretches of steep trail.

The Ride: Pick up the Upper Elk Spur Trail on the northwest corner of the day-use parking area, next to the orange gate. In 200 feet the ADA Trail goes off to the right, so turn here to ride the ADA Loop. The ADA Trail winds through dense forest of Douglas-firs, alders, and sword ferns for 1.5 miles before intersecting again with the Upper Elk Spur Trail. If you turn left at this junction you'll be back at the trailhead in 0.6 mile.

To ride the Peanut Loop, pick up the Upper Elk Spur Trail on the northwest corner of the day-use parking area. Follow it 1.9 miles, veering left at both junctions with the ADA Trail. When you reach the Doe Crossing Trail, turn left on it and ride for 0.5 mile. At the junction with the Holly Trail, turn left to stay on the Doe Crossing Trail. In another 0.4 mile, turn left again on the Lower Elk Spur Trail and ride it 1.4 miles back to the trailhead.

Donna on Zoey and Nancy on Sundance, cruising
along the Upper Elk Spur segment of the Peanut Loop.

Anvil Loop

Trailhead: Start at Sahara Creek Campground

Length: 12.5 miles round trip

Elevation: 1,500 to 3,000 feet, with total elevation gain of 2,400 feet

Difficulty: Challenging -- bridges, creek crossings, steep trail

Footing: Hoof protection suggested

Season: Summer through fall

Permits: Discover Pass required for day use or overnight camping

Facilities: Toilet, potable water, and ADA-accessible mounting ramp at the horse camp. Stock water is available on the trail.

Highlights: This loop runs through dense forest and through clear-cuts, with significant elevation gain and several stretches of steep switchbacks. You're rewarded for your climbing with splendid views of Mt. Rainier from the clear-cut areas above Beaver Creek Camp, on the east side of the Anvil Loop, and on the upper Bull Run Trail.

The Ride: Pick up the Upper Elk Spur Trail on the northwest corner of the day-use area. At both junctions with the ADA Trail, stay to the left and in 1.9 miles you'll reach the junction where the Doe Crossing

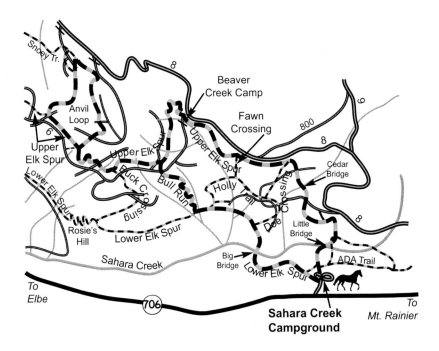

*Nancy on Sundance and Donna on Zoey and leading Tex, on the
Anvil Loop in a clear-cut with a panoramic view of Mt. Rainier.*

Trail goes off to the left. Stay to the right on the Upper Elk Spur Trail.
In 0.6 mile you'll pass the junction with the Fawn Crossing Trail, and
in another 0.8 mile you'll reach Beaver Creek Camp. This trailhead
boasts picnic tables, hitching rails, stock water, a vault toilet, and parking for several trailers. The Upper Elk Spur Trail continues up the
hill, and soon enters a clear-cut area with a view of Mt. Rainier. The
higher the trail climbs the more impressive the views get. Then the
trail traverses a ridge, passing the Bull Run Trail (this will be your
eventual return route) and the Buck Crossing Trail in the process.
About 0.6 mile past the junction with the Buck Crossing Trail you'll
reach the first intersection with the Anvil Loop Trail. Turn right on it
and you'll circle the flat top of a ridge that was recently clear-cut. The
views of Mt. Rainier from the east side of the loop are breathtaking.
After 2.2 miles, the trail loops back to intersect again with the Upper
Elk Spur Trail. Turn left and follow it 0.5 mile to the first Anvil Loop
junction, then continue on the Upper Elk Spur for 1.2 miles to the junction with the Bull Run Trail. Turn right on it, and follow the switchbacks down for 1.1 mile. (There are good views of Mt. Rainier from
the clear-cut in the upper section of this trail.) When you arrive at the
Lower Elk Spur Trail, turn left on it and follow it 2.1 miles back to the
horse camp.

Beaver Cr./Buck Crossing Loop

Trailhead: Start at Sahara Creek Campground
Length: 9.5 miles round trip
Elevation: 1,500 to 2,700 feet
Difficulty: Challenging -- bridges, creek crossings, steep trail
Footing: Hoof protection suggested
Season: Summer through fall
Permits: Discover Pass required for day use or overnight camping
Facilities: Toilet, potable water, and ADA-accessible mounting ramp at the horse camp. Stock water is available on the trail.

Highlights: This loop features panoramic views of Mt. Rainier from the switchbacks above Beaver Creek Camp, and runs through beautiful stands of maple trees and sword ferns on the Buck Crossing Trail.

The Ride: Pick up the Upper Elk Spur Trail on the northwest side of the day-use area. In the first 0.6 mile the two legs of the ADA Trail go off to your right. Then in another 1.3 miles the Doe Crossing Trail departs on your left, and 0.6 mile later the Fawn Crossing Trail also goes off to the left. In 0.9 mile after that you'll reach Beaver Creek Camp, where you'll find stock water, picnic tables, a toilet, and hitch-

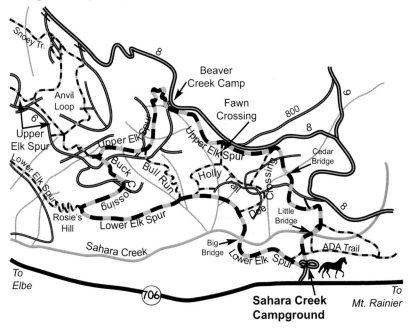

ing rails. Continue on the
Upper Elk Spur Trail for
another mile, during which
you'll ride through a clear-
cut with excellent views of
Mt. Rainier. At the junction
with the Bull Run Trail,
stay right and continue on
the Upper Elk Spur Trail
for another 0.6 mile. Turn
left at the junction with the
Buck Crossing Trail, which
features huge maple trees
and whole hillsides of
sword ferns. After 1.2 miles
of steady downhill travel,
turn left on the Lower Elk
Spur Trail and follow it 3.3
miles back to the trailhead.

*Nancy on Sundance and Donna
on Zoey, enjoying the lovely forest.*

*You'll have a great view of Mt. Rainier
from the clear-cut above Beaver Creek Camp.*

Holly/Fawn Loop

Trailhead:	Start at Sahara Creek Campground
Length:	5.5 miles round trip
Elevation:	1,500 to 2,150 feet
Difficulty:	Moderate -- bridges, steep trail
Footing:	Hoof protection suggested
Season:	Summer through fall
Permits:	Discover Pass required for day use or overnight camping
Facilities:	Toilet, potable water, and ADA-accessible mounting ramp at the horse camp. No stock water on the trail.

Highlights: Even though this is a relatively short trail, the elevation gain makes it a fairly strenuous ride. It's a fun loop that is longer and more challenging than the Peanut Loop, but it isn't as ambitious an undertaking as some of the longer trails in the area.

The Ride: For variety, we rode this loop in a clockwise direction. If you want to do the same, pick up the Lower Elk Spur Trail on the southwest corner of the day-use parking area, next to the orange gate.

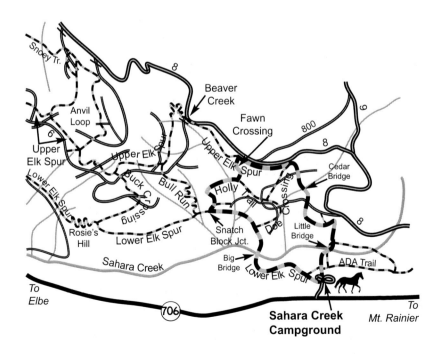

In 1.4 miles the Doe Crossing Trail goes off to the right. Continue 0.5 mile farther to the Snatch Block Junction and turn right on the Holly Trail. You'll head steadily uphill for 0.7 mile, then veer left on the Fawn Crossing Trail. It switchbacks upward for 0.3 mile before reaching the Upper Elk Spur Trail. Turn right here and follow the Upper Elk Spur for 2.5 miles back to the trailhead, moving steadily downward the entire time.

Nancy and Donna ride Sundance and Zoey through the forest.

At the Lower Elk Spur/Holly Trail junction you'll find a historic snatch block that was used to help cut and carry logs back in the heyday of logging via railroad.

Thimbleberry

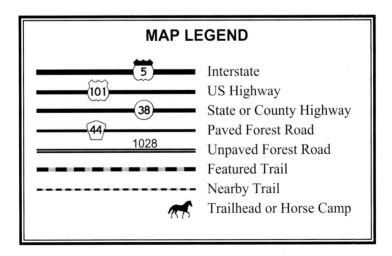

Scatter Creek

Private Timberland

Scatter Creek is a very pleasant year-round riding area on private timberland adjacent to the Scatter Creek Wildlife Area. The area offers dozens of miles of logging roads and single-track trails to explore and is easily accessible from I-5 just south of Olympia. You'll ride along the edge of the Scatter Creek Wildlife Area to reach the horse trails, but the wildlife area itself is off limits to protect several endangered species. The trails on the private forestland run up small hills and through shallow valleys. There are no scenic vistas, but the forest is quite varied, ranging from dense, shady stands of Douglas-fir and alder to recent clear-cuts. The roads and trails are not well signed, so bring your map, your compass or GPS, and your sense of adventure, and go exploring!

Karen and Vaquera lead the way along a trail at Scatter Creek.

Getting to Scatter Creek

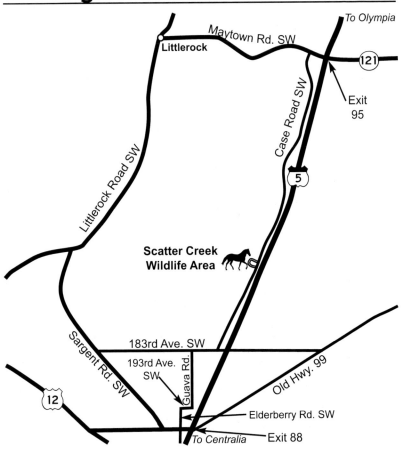

Scatter Creek Area Trails

Trail	Difficulty	Elevation	Round Trip
Scatter Creek Trails	Moderate	125-375	Varies

Scatter Creek Wildlife Area

Directions: From I-5 about 12 miles south of Olympia, take Exit 95 and go west toward the Farm Boy Restaurant. In 0.2 mile, turn south on Case Road SW. Watch your mileage carefully, and in exactly 4 miles turn right into an unsigned gravel parking loop. You'll see a kiosk on the far side of the parking area, next to a gray steel gate.

Elevation: 200 feet

Campsites: Overnight camping not permitted

Facilities: Parking for many trailers, no other facilities

Permits: Discover Pass required

Season: Year round

Contact: http://wdfw.wa.gov/lands/wildlife_areas/scatter_creek/, 360-902-2515

Karen pauses for a photo along a forest road,
while Vaquera has her eye on the roadside grass.

Scatter Creek Trails

Trailhead: Start at the Scatter Creek Wildlife Area Trailhead

Length: Varies depending on route taken

Elevation: 125 to 375 feet

Difficulty: Moderate -- some navigation skill needed because most roads and trails are not signed

Footing: Hoof protection recommended

Season: Year round -- gravel roads offer good footing year round, but single-track trails can be muddy and slippery when wet

Permits: Discover Pass required

Facilities: Parking for many trailers, but no other facilities. Stock water is available on the trail.

Highlights: You'll ride around the edge of the Scatter Creek Wildlife Area to get to the trails, but the riding is actually on forest land owned by Port Blakely, Weyerhauser, and Pope and Talbot, who have graciously granted permission to the public to horseback ride here. The

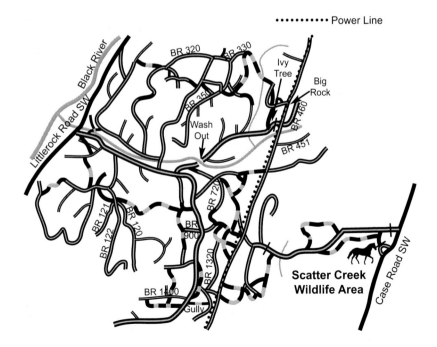

area is laced with gravel logging roads inter-connected by single-track trails that create many loop options. The gravel roads offer good footing year round, but the single-track trails can be muddy and slick after wet weather. Hunting is permitted in season.

The Ride: Ride around the steel gate on the west side of the parking area. Follow the horse trail signs north to a gravel road. Turn left on the gravel road or on the single-track trail that runs just to the left of it, and ride west along the edge of the wildlife area and into the woods. Your major landmarks include the power line that runs generally north and south and the creek that bisects the area from east to west. Pick a logging road or a trail to ride out on, and have fun exploring the forest!

Karen rides Vaquera off a gravel road onto a single-track trail leading into the woods.

Tex saunters along a gravel road.

Cape jewelweed

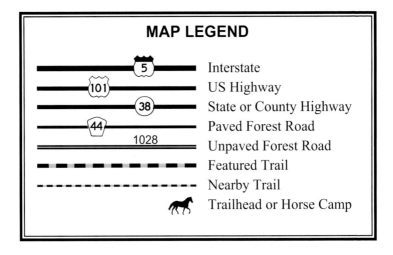

MAP LEGEND

5	Interstate
101	US Highway
38	State or County Highway
44	Paved Forest Road
1028	Unpaved Forest Road
— — —	Featured Trail
- - - -	Nearby Trail
🐎	Trailhead or Horse Camp

Tunerville Campground

Washington State Dept. of Natural Resources

Back in 1917, the Deep River Logging Camp had homes, shops, and even a dance hall. Today, nothing remains of the logging camp, but the area, now known as Tunerville Campground, has been used for decades as a camping spot and staging area for local riders who want an alternative to beach riding. In 1991, DNR and local volunteers put in corrals and other camping facilities, and recently volunteers raised funds for the installation of a vault toilet. Equestrians, hikers, mountain bike riders, ATV riders, and hunters share the nearby DNR forest roads and trails. Note that the Rayonier forest lands to the north and west of the campground are open to the public only during hunting season.

Moss-draped Douglas-firs line the trails around Tunerville Campground.

Getting to Tunerville

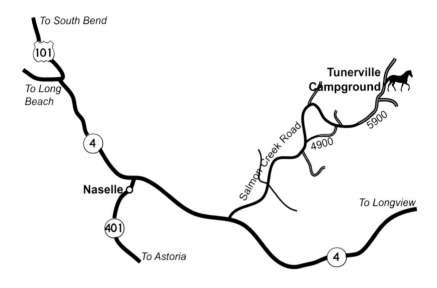

Tunerville's overnight accommodations include 3 corrals,
plus plenty of trees for highlining.

Tunerville Campground

Directions: From the junction of Hwy. 4 and Hwy. 401 near Naselle, go east on Hwy. 4 for 3.5 miles. Between mileposts 8 and 9, turn left on Salmon Creek Road, which eventually becomes Road 5900. Follow it 10.3 miles to the campground on the right. The road is paved except for the last 3.5 miles, which are gravel. **NOTE:** As of our publication date, Road 5900 was closed and a detour was available. Check with DNR before you go to find out about accessibility.

Elevation: 500 feet

Campsites: 3 parking spurs with 5 campsites. All sites have fire rings and some have picnic tables.

Facilities: Vault toilet, three corrals, several hitching rails, and plenty of trees for highlining. Stock water is available from Salmon Creek on the east edge of the campground.

Permits: Discover Pass required

Season: Early summer through fall

Contact: Pacific Cascade Region, Washington DNR, 360-577-2025

Tunerville Area Trails

Trail	Difficulty	Elevation	Round Trip
Tunerville Area Trails	Moderate	350-1,000	Varies

Tunerville Area Trails

Trailhead: Start at Tunerville Horse Camp

Length: Varies by route selected

Elevation: 350 to 1,000 feet

Difficulty: Easy to moderate

Footing: Hoof protection recommended for gravel roads

Season: Early summer through fall

Permits: Discover Pass required

Facilities: Toilet and stock water at the horse camp. Stock water is available on the trail.

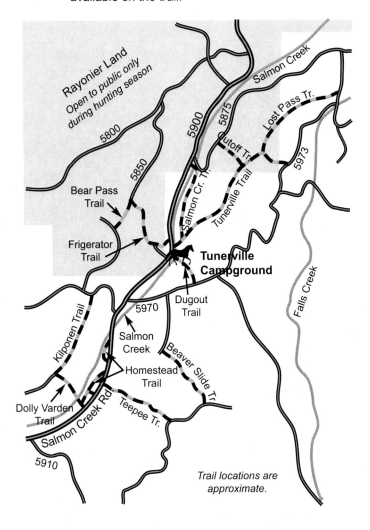

Trail locations are approximate.

*Teresa rides Pops and Lydia rides Magic
down a forest road near Tunerville Campground.*

Highlights: There aren't any "official" DNR trails out of Tunerville Horse Camp, but there are plenty of forest roads and user-created trails to explore in this beautiful area. The trails are maintained entirely by volunteers, so depending on the number of downed trees and the number of volunteers available, some trails may not be cleared every year.

The Ride: The Tunerville Trail departs on the east side of Road 5900, about 100 feet past the northern-most horse campsite at Tunerville. The Frigerator Trail departs on the west side of Road 5900, a little farther up the road. The Dugout Trail heads east from the horse camp and crosses Salmon Creek. The Homestead Trail departs on the west side of Road 5900 about 0.7 mile south of the camp, and if you continue traveling down Salmon Creek Road you'll see the Teepee Trail on the east and the Dolly Varden Trail on the west. All of these trails connect with forest roads and/or other trails so you can make a variety of loops in the surrounding hills. Have fun exploring!

Piggy-back plant

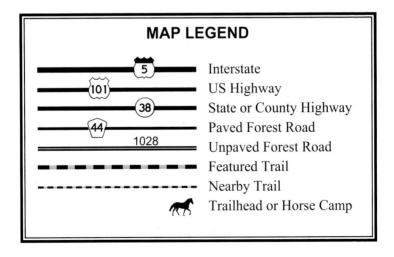

Walupt
Horse Camp

Gifford Pinchot National Forest

Walupt Lake is situated on the scenic southern edge of the Goat Rocks Wilderness. Yakama Indian legend says the wild dogs that live in the bottom of Walupt Lake will attack you if you turn your back on the lake. Whether the legend is true or not, the lake is so pretty that you wouldn't want to turn your back on it anyway.

Walupt Horse Camp, located about a mile from the lake, provides access to trails that explore the high ridges around the lake. Many of the trails involve significant elevation gains, but the trails aren't terribly steep and there aren't many steep side hills. You have the option of making some long loops or doing shorter out-and-back rides. Either way, in clear weather you'll enjoy some beautiful mountain views along the way.

Walupt Lake

Getting to Walupt Horse Camp

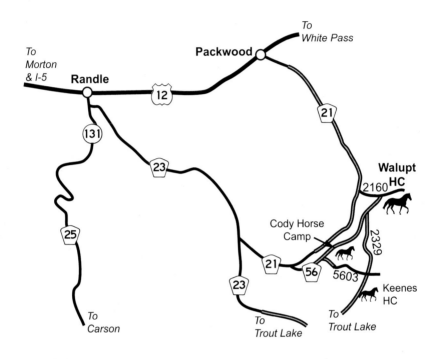

Many sites at Walupt Horse Camp are double-size pull-throughs.

Walupt Horse Camp

Directions: From I-5, take Exit 68 (Yakima/White Pass) and head east on Hwy. 12. After 48.5 miles, turn right on Hwy. 131 in Randle. In 1 mile, when the road makes a Y, veer left on Road 23. Follow it for 17.7 miles, then turn left on Forest Road 21 and continue 12.7 miles. Turn right on Road 2160 and drive 3.8 miles to the campground on the right. **NOTE:** As of our publication date, Road 23 was closed due to a washout. Check with the Forest Service for access information before you make plans to visit.

Elevation: 3900 feet

Campsites: 9 sites with highline poles, fire pits, and picnic tables. Five sites are double sites. All sites but 2 are pull-throughs. Some sites have only 1 highline pole, so you may need to bring tree-savers to connect your highline to one of the many trees in your campsite. Most sites are fairly level.

Facilities: Vault toilets, manure bins, garbage cans, and potable water from a hand pump. The day-use area, which has parking for 4-5 trailers, is located on Road 2160 just past the entrance to the horse camp.

Permits: Camping fee

Season: Late June through mid-September

Contact: Cowlitz Valley Ranger District, 360-497-1100

Walupt Area Trails

Trail	Difficulty	Elevation	Round Trip
Chambers Lake	Challenging	3,400-4,550	10 miles
Coleman Weedpatch Loop	Challenging	3,700-5,650	16 miles
Midway Meadows Loop	Challenging	3,800-5,200	17 miles
Nannie Ridge/Sheep Lake	Challenging	3,900-6,100	8-12 miles

Chambers Lake

Trailhead: Start at Walupt Horse Camp
Length: 10 miles round trip
Elevation: 3,400 to 4,550 feet
Difficulty: Challenging -- bridge, challenging river crossing
Footing: Hoof protection recommended
Season: Summer through fall
Permits: Camping fee, no fee for day-use parking
Facilities: Toilet, potable water, and manure bins at the horse camp. Parking for 4-5 trailers in the day-use area. Stock water is available on the trail.

Highlights: This trail weaves in and out of the Goat Rocks Wilderness, ending at a lake that you could drive to if you were so inclined. Nonetheless, it's a beautiful trail. Several people we met at other horse camps in the area told us this ride is one of their all-time favorites. However, when we rode it the weather was pouring rain for the fourth

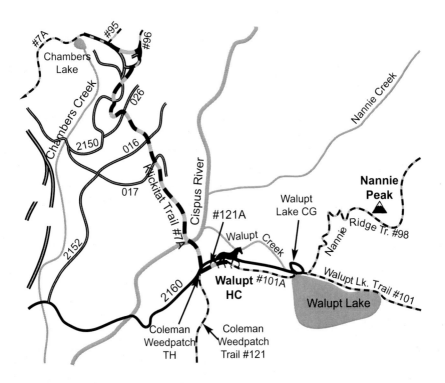

day in a row (in August!), so we didn't make it all the way to Chambers Lake. While we got soaking wet in spite of our rain gear, we can attest that the trails in the Walupt Lake area are not slick or muddy even after heavy rains.

The Ride: Pick up the Coleman Weedpatch Trail #121A next to campsite 1 and follow it 0.7 mile to the Coleman Weedpatch hiker trailhead on Road 2160. Cross Road 2160 and pick up the Klickitat Trail #7A on the other side. It heads steadily downhill for 0.8 mile to the very rocky shore of the Cispus River. When the river first comes into view you may be tempted to ride out to it, but instead veer left and stay on the trail. It will take you to a good fording spot a little downstream, indicated by several rock cairns on the south side of the river and more cairns on a log on a sandbar in the middle of the river. After crossing the river, the trail goes steadily uphill, mostly on single-track trail but at times on old forest roads. The forest is beautiful, with hemlocks, incense cedars, and Douglas-firs in the canopy, and bear grass, vine maples, bracken ferns, and huckleberries beneath. We sincerely hope you experience better weather when you ride this trail than we did!

*Lydia rides Magic along the rocky shore of
the Cispus River before fording the river.*

Coleman Weedpatch Loop

Trailhead:	Start at Walupt Horse Camp
Length:	16 miles round trip
Elevation:	3,700 to 5,650 feet
Difficulty:	Challenging -- steep in places, with a few steep dropoffs and sidehills
Footing:	Hoof protection recommended -- the trail is very rocky in places
Season:	Summer through fall
Permits:	Camping fee, no fee for day-use parking
Facilities:	Toilet, potable water, and manure bins at the horse camp. Parking for 4-5 trailers in the day-use area. Stock water is available on the trail.

Highlights: Coleman Weedpatch is a series of grassy meadows along the PCT that are filled with seasonal wildflowers. Located near the halfway point along the loop, the meadows make a nice lunch spot for you and your horse. As you travel the loop, you'll enjoy beautiful forest, small meadows and ponds, and occasional peek-a-boo views of the surrounding ridges. This loop also has some steep stretches, some very rocky stretches, and a couple of steep side hills. If your horse is in good condition, though, it's a beautiful ride.

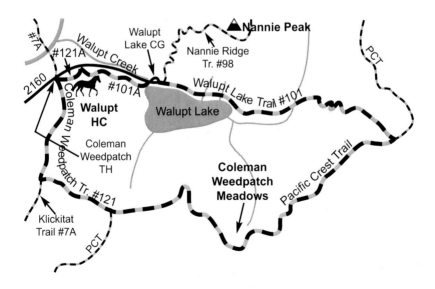

The Ride: Pick up the Coleman Weedpatch Trail #121A next to campsite 1 and follow it 0.7 mile to the Coleman Weedpatch hiker trailhead on Road 2160. Continue on the Coleman Weedpatch Trail #121 for 1.8 miles, gaining elevation steadily. When the Klickitat Trail #7A comes in on the right, stay left on the Coleman Weedpatch Trail. In 1.1 miles, veer left on the PCT. You'll continue gaining elevation for the next 1.3 miles. Then the trail descends 600 feet in 1.4 miles, passes the Coleman Weedpatch meadows, and levels out. About 3.6 miles after you pass the Coleman Weedpatch you'll reach the junction with the Walupt Lake Trail #101. Turn left here. For the next 2 miles the trail heads steeply downhill on a rocky, eroded trail, losing nearly 1,000 feet of elevation. The trail levels out after that, and about a mile later you'll catch sight of Waldo Lake. The trail traverses the hillside above the lake for a little more than a mile, to the junction with the Nannie Ridge Trail #98. Stay left, and in 500 feet you'll come out at the hiker trailhead and campground at Walupt Lake. Veer left and follow the white hoofprints painted on the pavement for 0.2 mile to a designated horse watering spot just outside the trailhead parking area. Next to the entrance sign for Walupt Campground, pick up Trail #101A and it will take you the last mile back to the horse camp.

Connie on Moose, Lydia on Magic, and Theresa on Sky, enjoying a lunch break at one of the Coleman Weedpatch meadows.

Midway Meadows Loop

Trailhead: Start at Walupt Lake Horse Camp

Length: 17 miles round trip

Elevation: 3,800 to 5,200 feet

Difficulty: Challenging -- significant elevation gain, a few steep side hills

Footing: Hoof protection recommended

Season: Summer through fall

Permits: Camping fee, no fee for day-use parking

Facilities: Toilet, potable water, and manure bins at the horse camp. Parking for 4-5 trailers in the day-use area. Stock water is available on the trail.

Highlights: This ride is rather long and has significant elevation gains in the first 3.5 miles, but after that the elevation changes are minor. The mountain views and beautiful terrain are a delight. Midway

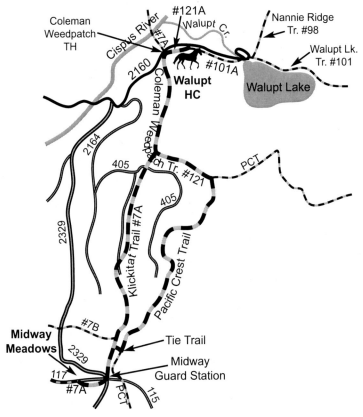

Meadows is a nice place for your horse to graze while you have lunch, and the Midway Guard Station is an interesting stop beside the trail.

The Ride: Pick up the Coleman Weedpatch Trail #121A next to campsite 1 and follow it 0.7 mile to the hiker trailhead on Road 2160, then continue on the Coleman Weedpatch Trail #121. It steadily gains elevation, and after 1.8 miles the Klickitat Trail #7A comes in on the right. This will be your return route, so for now stay to the left on the Coleman Weedpatch Trail. The trail continues climbing for another 1.1 mile, gaining a total of 1,400 feet of elevation since leaving the horse camp. At the junction with the PCT, turn right. The PCT gradually descends, losing about 600 feet of elevation in the next 4 miles. Near Midway Meadows, watch for an unsigned 50-foot tie trail on the right that will take you to the Klickitat Trail #7A. Turn left on the Klickitat Trail and continue 0.9 mile to the Midway Guard Station. After the trail crosses Roads 2329 and 117, continue on the Klickitat Trail for 0.5 mile to Midway Meadows. After enjoying the meadows, return to the guard station and retrace your steps on the Klickitat Trail. This time, ignore the tie trail to the PCT and stay on the Klickitat Trail. In 0.3 mile after you pass the tie trail you'll pass Trail #7B on the left. Stay to the right and continue 3.5 miles to the junction with the Coleman Weedpatch Trail, with little elevation change along the way. Turn left on the Coleman Weedpatch Trail and retrace your steps to the horse camp.

You'll find a good horse-watering spot just behind the
Midway Guard Station, near Midway Meadows.

Nannie Ridge & Sheep Lake

Trailhead: Start at Walupt Horse Camp

Length: 8 miles round trip to the Nannie Ridge saddle, 9 miles round trip to Nannie Peak, 12 miles round trip to Sheep Lake

Elevation: 3,900 to 5,900 feet to the Nannie Ridge saddle or to Sheep Lake; 3,900 to 6,100 feet to Nannie Peak

Difficulty: Challenging -- steep trail to the Nannie Ridge saddle; a couple of steep side hills along Nannie Ridge

Footing: Hoof protection recommended — trail has rocky stretches

Season: Summer through fall

Permits: Camping fee, no fee for day use parking

Facilities: Toilet, potable water, and manure bins at the horse camp. Parking for 4-5 trailers in the day-use area. Stock water is available on the trail.

Highlights: Panoramic mountain views await you from Nannie Peak and Nannie Ridge (both reportedly named for a mule, not a goat), and Sheep Lake is a sub-alpine gem surrounded by flower-filled meadows. Your horse will need to be in good condition, though, because the trail between Walupt Lake and the Nannie Ridge saddle is an unrelenting uphill trek. After you pass Nannie Peak, the trail is a series of gentle ups and downs until you reach Sheep Lake.

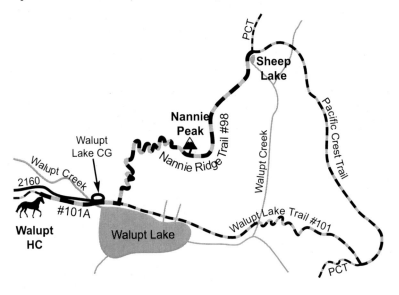

Tex heads through the huckleberries along the Nannie Peak Trail.

The Ride: Pick up the trail at the kiosk between campsites 3 and 4, turn left on the campground loop trail, then at the next junction turn right on Trail #101A to Walupt Lake. In about a mile the trail comes out at the Walupt Lake Campground sign, next to the designated horse watering spot. Follow the white hoofprints painted on the campground road to reach the Walupt Lake Trail #101. Follow it for 500 feet, then turn left on the Nannie Ridge Trail #98. This trail gains 2,000 feet of elevation in the next 2.5 miles, with no steep side hills but some significant step-ups over rocks and tree roots. You'll get a view of Mt. St. Helens in this section. Finally, you'll reach a level open spot. An unofficial 0.5-mile spur trail to the top of Nannie Peak goes to off to the left. If you follow it, you'll be rewarded with panoramic views of Mt. Adams, Mt. St. Helens, Mt. Rainier, and the Goat Rocks. Continue on the Nannie Ridge Trail for 2 more miles to Sheep Lake, a pretty little lake surrounded by meadows.

Bonus Loop: To complete a 17-mile loop with elevations of 3,900 to 5,900 feet, continue past Sheep Lake to the PCT and turn right. Follow it as it traverses a steep ridge (with some steep side hills along the way) that offers some amazing mountain views. After 4.2 miles, turn right on the Walupt Lake Trail #101 and follow this rocky trail downhill for 5.7 miles to return to the horse camp.

Avalanche lily

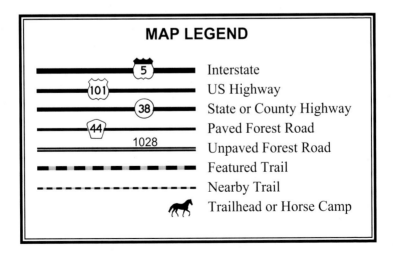

MAP LEGEND

Interstate
US Highway
State or County Highway
Paved Forest Road
Unpaved Forest Road
Featured Trail
Nearby Trail
Trailhead or Horse Camp

White Pass Horse Camp

Okanogan-Wenatchee National Forest

White Pass Horse Camp, located just off Hwy. 12 at the crest of the Cascades, provides access to two spectacular wilderness areas. On the north side of Hwy. 12, the William O. Douglas Wilderness (named for the Supreme Court justice who championed conservation issues and had a home nearby) has moderate terrain, dense forest, huckleberry meadows, and many small lakes. On the south side of Hwy. 12, the Goat Rocks Wilderness features steep ridges, wildflower/huckleberry meadows, rugged terrain, and spectacular mountain views. White Pass has more variety in the trails than you'll find at most horse camps. There is something here for everyone.

Shelley and Donna on Johnnie Walker and Star, on a stretch of the Cowlitz Trail in the William O. Douglas Wilderness.

Getting to White Pass

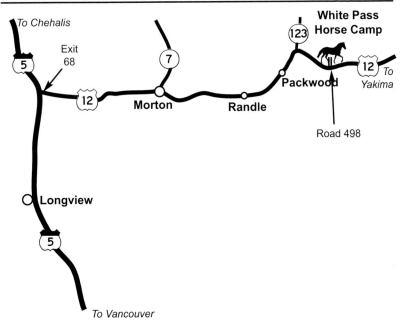

*Johnnie Walker and Star relax on their
highline at White Pass Horse Camp.*

White Pass Horse Camp

Directions: From I-5, take Exit 68 (Yakima/White Pass) and drive east on Hwy. 12 for 85 miles. Just past the White Pass Winter Recreation Area, turn left on Road 498. Take the first right to enter the horse camp.

Elevation: 4,450 feet

Campsites: 6 sites with room for one trailer each. All sites are level, with hitching posts and trees for highlining. A couple of sites have fire rings, and a couple of others have picnic tables. Several additional overflow camping spots have hitching rails and trees for highlining.

Facilities: Vault toilet. Stock water is available from a creek about 0.1 mile away. The large day-use parking area has 7 hitching rails and a couple of picnic tables, and can hold 10 trailers. Because of the camp's proximity to Hwy. 12, you may hear some road noise.

Permits: Northwest Forest Pass required for camping or day use

Season: Summer through fall

Contact: Naches Ranger District, 509-653-1401

Note: In the William O. Douglas Wilderness, your party size is limited to 12 "heartbeats" (including people, horses, and dogs). Example: 5 people + 5 horses + 2 dogs = 12 heartbeats.

White Pass Area Trails

Trail	Difficulty	Elevation	Round Trip
Deer and Sand Lakes	Moderate	4,450-5,350	6 miles
Dumbell Lake Loop	Moderate	4,300-5,600	14.5 miles
Leech Lake Loop	Easy	4,500-4,600	2 miles
Pigtail Peak	Moderate	4,450-6,000	8 miles
Shellrock Lake Trail Loop	Challenging	4,300-5,600	18 miles
Shoe Lake	Difficult	4,550-6,600	15 miles

Deer and Sand Lakes

Trailhead: Start at White Pass Horse Camp

Length: 6 miles round trip

Elevation: 4,450 to 5,350 feet

Difficulty: Moderate

Footing: Hoof protection recommended

Season: Summer through fall

Permits: Northwest Forest Pass required

Facilities: Toilet and stock water at the horse camp. Stock water is available on the trail.

Highlights: This trail takes you through dense forest to pretty Deer Lake and tiny Sand Lake. It's a nice out-and-back ride for your first or last day in camp, or for a day when you want a break from the longer rides in the area.

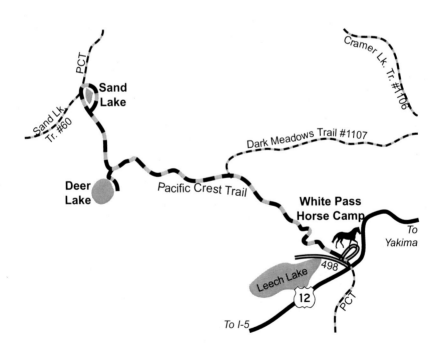

Johnnie Walker gazes out across Deer Lake.

Photo courtesy of Shelley Seidenverg

The Ride: Pick up the northbound PCT at the hiker parking area just west of the horse camp. In 1.3 miles, the Dark Meadows Trail goes off to the right. Stay left on the PCT. In another mile an unsigned user trail goes to the left. Follow it, and it will take you to the shore of Deer Lake. After enjoying the view, return to the PCT and turn left, and in 0.6 mile you'll be at Sand Lake. Its sandy shores provide easy access for your horse to get a drink, and if you look closely you may find evidence of the presence of elk nearby. Retrace your steps to return to the horse camp in 3 miles.

Dumbell Lake Loop

Trailhead: Start at White Pass Horse Camp
Length: 14.5 miles round trip
Elevation: 4,300 to 5,600 feet
Difficulty: Moderate, though a short stretch of the Cramer Lake Trail traverses a steep and rocky side hill
Footing: Hoof protection a must
Season: Summer through fall
Permits: Northwest Forest Pass required
Facilities: Toilet and stock water at the horse camp. Stock water is available on the trail.

Highlights: This fun loop is shorter than the Shellrock Lake Trail Loop, and it takes you to Dumbell Lake, the largest lake in this end of the Wilderness.

The Ride: Since we rode the Shellrock Lake Trail Loop in a counterclockwise direction, we opted to ride this loop clockwise. Pick up the

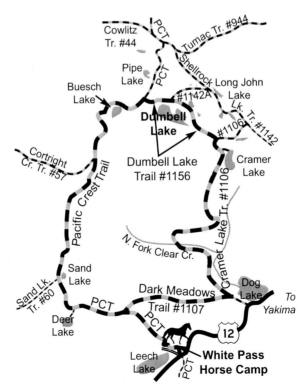

northbound PCT at the hiker parking area just west of the horse camp. In 1.3 miles the Dark Meadows Trail goes off to the right. Stay left on the PCT. In another mile an unsigned user trail goes to the left to Deer Lake. Stay right. In 0.6 mile the Sand Lake Trail #60 goes to the left. Again stay right. In 2.0 miles, the Cortright Creek Trail #57 goes to the left. Yet again, you'll stay to the right. In 1.3 miles you'll pass Buesch Lake, and 0.4 mile later you'll reach the junction with the Dumbell Lake Trail #1156. Turn right on it, and in 0.3 mile you'll come to Dumbell Lake. In another 0.1 mile the Long John Lake Trail #1142A goes off to the left. Stay to the right on the Dumbell Lake Trail. In 0.9 mile, turn right on the Cramer Lake Trail #1106. Follow it downhill for 2.1 miles, ford the North Fork of Clear Creek and continue 1.6 miles to the junction with the Dark Meadows Trail #1107. Going straight at this intersection just takes you to the people campground at Dog Lake, so turn right and follow the Dark Meadows Trail for 1.8 miles to the junction with the PCT. Turn left on the PCT to return to the horse camp in 1.3 miles.

Shelley on Johnnie Walker and Donna on Star,
at Sand Lake on the PCT.

Leech Lake Loop

Trailhead: Start at White Pass Horse Camp
Length: 2 miles round trip
Elevation: 4,500 to 4,600 feet
Difficulty: Easy -- two bridges to cross
Footing: Hoof protection recommended
Season: Summer through fall
Permits: Northwest Forest Pass required
Facilities: Toilet and stock water at the horse camp.

Highlights: If you're looking for an easy jaunt to stretch your horse's legs, or you want to take a leisurely walk after dinner, this is the trail for you. It follows old gravel roads all the way around Leech Lake, providing views of the lake from the east and west ends. The rest of the route is forested.

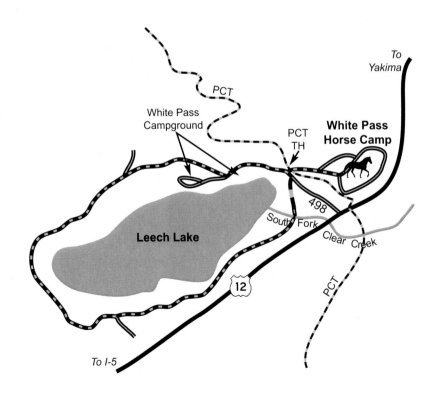

Top: The trail runs mostly through the forest.
Middle: The west part of the loop runs across a rockslide.
Bottom: The view of Leech Lake from the rockslide.

The Ride: From the horse camp, ride out to Road 498 and turn left. In about 100 feet, turn right on a wide path that takes you over a bridge across the South Fork of Clear Creek. You'll now be on an old gravel road. In 0.6 mile the road splits. Veer right here. Soon the road crosses a rock slide that provides an unobstructed view of the lake and the hills to the east. After 0.6 mile the road splits again. Veer right again, and in 0.3 mile the trail comes out on the campground road for the White Pass Campground. Turn left here and follow the camp-ground road past the PCT hiker parking area to the entrance to the horse camp.

Pigtail Peak

Trailhead: Start at White Pass Horse Camp

Length: 8 miles round trip

Elevation: 4,450 to 6,000 feet

Difficulty: Moderate -- significant elevation gain

Footing: Hoof protection recommended

Season: Summer through fall

Permits: Northwest Forest Pass required

Facilities: Toilet and stock water at the horse camp. Stock water is available on the trail.

Highlights: It's a big climb to the summit of Pigtail Peak, the apex of the chairlift system for the White Pass Winter Recreation Area. But

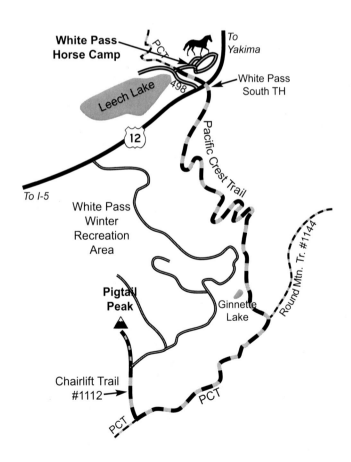

you'll be richly rewarded for the exertion, with beautiful wildflower meadows in season and spectacular views of Mt. Rainier from the top.

The Ride: From the horse camp, ride the PCT or Road 498 out to Hwy. 12 and cross it. Continue on the PCT next to the trail kiosk at the White Pass South Trailhead. For the first 2 miles, the trail switchbacks up a fairly steep ridge, gaining nearly 1,000 feet of elevation. Then the trail levels out a bit and passes Ginnette Lake on the right. In this stretch the trail runs through meadows filled with huckleberries, white rhododendrons, and a dazzling display of seasonal wildflowers. After another 1.3 miles, turn right on the Chairlift Trail #1112. In 0.3 mile, it will take you to a gravel road. Ride uphill on this road for 0.2 mile to reach the summit of Pigtail Peak. Holy cow! The 270-degree panoramic view is breathtaking. You'll see Mt. Rainier, so close you can almost reach out and touch it. The entire William O. Douglas Wilderness is laid out at your feet, and mountains march off into the distance to the north, west, and east. The view is marred somewhat by the ski lifts in the way, but the presence of the ski lifts is what gives you relatively easy access to this million-dollar view. Retrace your steps to return to your trailer.

Shelley on Johnnie Walker and Donna on Star, at the summit of Pigtail Peak with Mt. Rainier in the background.

Shellrock Lake Trail Loop

Trailhead: Start at White Pass Horse Camp

Length: 18 miles round trip

Elevation: 4,300 to 5,600 feet

Difficulty: Challenging -- long trail, with a short segment that traverses a steep, rocky hillside. Otherwise, this trail is moderate.

Footing: Hoof protection recommended

Season: Summer through fall

Permits: Northwest Forest Pass required

Facilities: Toilet and stock water at the horse camp. Stock water is available on the trail.

Highlights: This ride doesn't go to Shellrock Lake, but instead gets its name from the trail that allows you to make a longer loop than the Dumbell Loop ride. While the north/south legs of the loop are heavily forested and have significant elevation changes, the Shellrock Lake

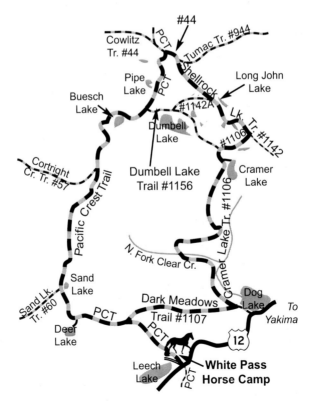

*Shelley and Donna ride Johnnie Walker and Star through
the beautiful meadows along the Shellrock Lake Trail.*

Trail segment runs across fairly level terrain, through open forest, past dozens of small lakes, and through meadows of huckleberries and wildflowers.

The Ride: Pick up the northbound PCT at the hiker parking area just west of the horse camp. In 1.3 miles, turn right on the Dark Meadows Trail #1107. In 1.8 miles you'll reach the junction with the Cramer Lake Trail #1106. In 1.6 miles you'll ford the North Fork of Clear Creek, and after 2 miles of climbing you'll catch sight of Cramer Lake. The lake shore is boggy and isn't a safe watering spot, so ignore the spur trail on the right that leads to the north end of the lake. Continue on the trail for 0.2 mile, and at the junction where the Dumbell Lake Trail #1156 goes to the left, stay right. In 0.6 mile you'll reach the Shellrock Lake Trail #1142. Go left here and follow it through huckleberry meadows and past tiny lakes. In 0.9 mile you'll come to an unsigned junction. To the left is the Long John Lake Trail #1142A, which leads to Dumbell Lake. Veer right, and in another 0.9 mile turn left at the junction with the Cowlitz Trail #44. Enjoy the great view of Mt. Rainier, and in 0.1 mile turn left on the PCT. In 0.6 mile you'll find a good horse-watering spot at Pipe Lake. Follow the PCT 7.2 miles back to your trailer, staying to the left at all trail junctions except the Dark Meadows Trail, where you'll go to the right.

Shoe Lake

Trailhead: Start at White Pass Horse Camp
Length: 15 miles round trip
Elevation: 4,450 to 6,600 feet, with total elevation gain of 2,550 feet
Difficulty: Difficult -- steep side hills, big elevation gain
Footing: Hoof protection a must -- very rocky trail
Season: Summer through fall
Permits: Northwest Forest Pass required
Facilities: Toilet and stock water at the horse camp. Stock water is available on the trail.

Highlights: If you don't like heights, this is probably not the ride for you. But if your horse is in good shape and you don't mind steep side hills, go for it. The views of Mt. Rainier and the Goat Rocks are stunning, and Shoe Lake is a delightful lunch spot.

The Ride: From the horse camp, ride the PCT or Road 498 out to Hwy. 12 and cross it. Continue on the PCT next to the trail kiosk at

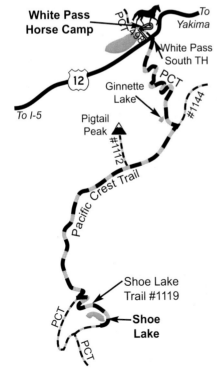

Above: The trail across the cirque into the Shoe Lake Basin. Below: Shoe Lake.

the White Pass South Trailhead. For the first 2 miles, the trail switch-backs up a fairly steep ridge, gaining nearly 1,000 feet of elevation. Then the trail levels out a bit and passes Ginnette Lake on the right. In this stretch, the trail runs through open areas filled with huckleberries, white rhododendrons, and a dazzling display of seasonal wildflowers. After another 1.3 miles, the Chairlift Trail #1112 goes off to the right. Stay left on the PCT, and in 1.9 miles the trail begins traversing a large cirque. You don't gain much elevation in the next mile as you cross this very steep and rocky side hill. (We got off and walked our horses.) Then the trail makes one switchback to bring you up over the saddle leading into the Shoe Lake Basin. Cowabunga! The Goat Rocks are on the southern skyline, with aquamarine Shoe Lake in the basin below you. It's breathtaking! In a few hundred feet the Shoe Lake Trail #1119 goes to the left. Turn here and follow it. (While you can make a loop around Shoe Lake via the PCT, don't be tempted. This stretch of the PCT includes a traverse across a big rockslide that has many places that could catch a horse's foot or break its leg.) Follow the Shoe Lake Trail down to the south end of the lake and have lunch on its beautiful shore. Then retrace your steps so you avoid the treacherous rockslide on the PCT as you return to your trailer.

Shelley and Donna on Johnnie Walker and Star on the saddle above the Shoe Lake Basin, with the Goat Rocks on the horizon.

Western pasque flower that has gone to seed.
(Also known as old man of the mountain.)

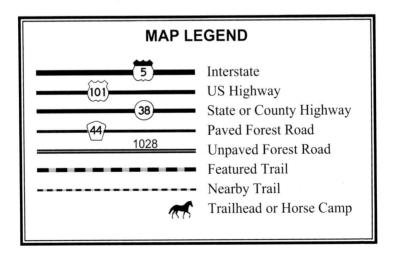

MAP LEGEND

⑤	Interstate
⑩⑴	US Highway
㊳	State or County Highway
㊹	Paved Forest Road
1028	Unpaved Forest Road
	Featured Trail
	Nearby Trail
🐎	Trailhead or Horse Camp

Willapa Hills Trail

Washington State Parks Department

The 56-mile long Willapa Hills Trail follows the right-of-way of the old Northern Pacific Railroad South Bend Branch from Chehalis to South Bend. The 27-mile stretch from Chehalis to Pe Ell has been improved and is accessible for horses, offering pleasant year-round, low-elevation riding. The Chehalis, Adna, Rainbow Falls, and Pe Ell Trailheads all have parking for horse trailers. From Chehalis to Adna the trail is paved, with a gravel path for horses beside it. Between Adna and Pe Ell the tread is compacted gravel. Because the trail is wide and fairly straight, you can see mountain bike riders and hikers coming a long way off. And because there is little elevation gain, bike riders won't be going very fast. In the summer there may be more exciting places to ride. But in winter when other trails are muddy and slick, the Willapa Hills Trail is mighty appealing.

Tex moves out along the Willapa Hills Trail near Rainbow Falls State Park, where the tread is packed gravel.

281

Getting to the Willapa Hills Trail

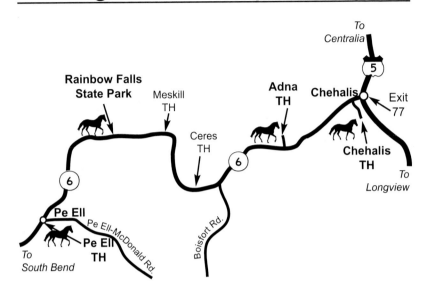

The Chehalis Trailhead has parking for 8 trailers.

Willapa Hills Trailheads

CHEHALIS TRAILHEAD

Directions: From I-5, take Exit 77 in Chelalis and drive west on Hwy. 6. At the first stoplight, turn left on Riverside Drive. In 0.2 mile, veer left on Newaukum Drive, drive 0.2 mile, and turn left on SW Sylvenus. Follow it for 0.1 mile, and turn right on Hillberger Road, then continue 0.5 mile to the trailhead. Trailer parking is on the left.

More Info: Toilet, parking for 8 trailers, open year round. No fee.

ADNA TRAILHEAD

Directions: From I-5, take Exit 77 in Chehalis and drive west on Hwy. 6. In 5 miles, turn right on Bunker Hill Road. In another 0.1 mile, turn right on Dieckman Road. The trailer parking area is on the right.

More Info: This trailhead offers parking for many trailers. Open year round. No fee.

RAINBOW FALLS STATE PARK TRAILHEAD

Directions: From I-5, take Exit 77 in Chehalis and drive west on Hwy. 6. Continue 17.3 miles. Turn right on Chandler Road, and in 0.3 mile turn right on Leudinghaus Road. Follow it for 0.8 mile and turn right into the park. Veer left and follow the sign that says "Day Use." Drive past the horse camp (no day-use parking there). According to park officials, you can ignore the sign that says "No Horses Beyond This Point" and park in the gravel lot adjacent to the picnic area. Please pick up your manure here, so equestrians' special parking privileges don't get revoked.

More Info: Rainbow Falls State Park has a toilet, picnic facilities, and parking for several trailers. It also has a 3-site horse camp with hitching rails, a vault toilet, stock water from a hand pump, picnic tables, and fire pits. Fee for overnight camping, or Discover Pass required for day use. Open year round.

PE ELL TRAILHEAD

Directions: From I-5, take Exit 77 in Chehalis and drive west on Hwy. 6 for 23 miles. In Pe Ell, go left on 4th St. The parking lot is ahead in 1 block.

More Info: This trailhead has a toilet, potable water spigots, hitching rails, ADA mounting ramp, a big turnaround area, and parking for 8 trailers. Open year round. No fee.

Willapa Hills Trail

Trailhead: Start at the Chehalis, Adna, Rainbow Falls State Park, or Pe Ell Trailheads

Length: Up to 54 miles round trip

Elevation: 200 to 450 feet

Difficulty: Easy

Footing: Hoof protection suggested

Season: Year round

Permits: See prior page

Facilities: See prior page. No stock water on the trail.

Highlights: The Willapa Hills Trail runs by pleasant woodlands, pastures, and working farmland as it roughly parallels the Chehalis River. The bridges that were washed out by winter floods several years ago have now been replaced, so you can ride all the way from Chehalis to Pe Ell. The Washington State Parks Dept. is working on funding to improve the trail west of Pe Ell, so watch for further developments.

The Ride: You can ride out and back from any of the 4 trailheads that have room for trailers. Or you can do a one way ride with a trailer

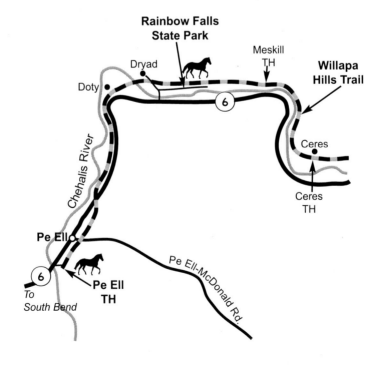

shuttle. (Drop off trailer #1 at one trailhead, use trailer #2 to drive the horses to another trailhead, ride to trailer #1, and use it to take you and the horses back to trailer #2). Note that at Rainbow Falls State Park, you'll take a connector trail across Leudinghaus Road to reach the Willapa Hills Trail.

The trail from Chehalis to Adna is paved, with a gravel path beside it for horses.

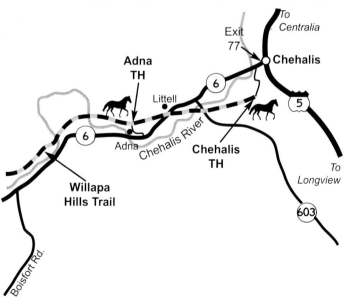

Snowberry

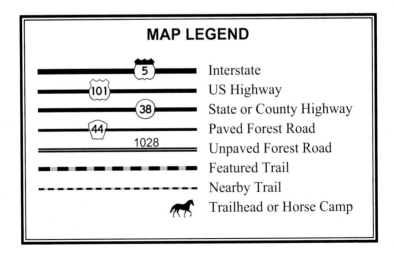

Wright Meadow

Gifford Pinchot National Forest

Wright Meadow isn't for everyone. You'll be primitive camping, with no water, no corrals, and no toilet. The riding is challenging, with big elevation changes and some steep side hills. The trails are rutted by motorcycles into a deep V in places, and erosion has exposed many roots your horse will have to clamber over. And though these trails are open to hikers, horses, and motorcycles, you'll encounter several steep traverses where it may be difficult to get off the trail if you were to meet an oncoming motorcycle. That said, the mountain views are breathtaking, the wildflowers in season are stunning, and the waterfalls are beautiful. We came here because the nearby Lewis River Horse Camp wasn't a viable option: the Quartz Creek Trail heading one direction from the horse camp is not horse friendly, and the Lewis River Trail heading the other direction was closed to stock use because several bridges had washed out. Plus, the Lewis River Horse Camp is a long way from what we had heard were the best trails in the area -- the trails on the uplands above the river valley. So Wright Meadow may be your best option here if you don't mind primitive camping and your horse is sure-footed and in good condition. If you go during the week, you may be able to avoid the motorcycles.

Mt. Adams from the Wright Meadows Trail.

287

Getting to Wright Meadow

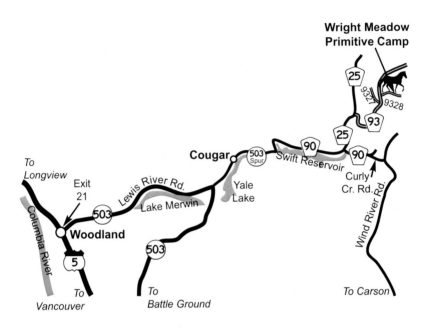

*The primitive camping area near Wright Meadows has
no facilities, but it can accommodate many trailers.*

Primitive Camping near Wright Mdw.

Directions: From Woodland, take Exit 21 from I-5 and go east on Hwy. 503/Lewis River Road toward Cougar. In 23 miles, Hwy. 503 turns to the right. Go straight on Hwy. 503-Spur, which becomes Road 90, for 23.7 miles.
From Carson, take the Wind River Hwy. north for 27.5 miles and turn left on Curly Creek Road. Follow it for 5.1 miles, then veer left on Road 90 and continue 4 miles.
All, Turn north on Road 25 and drive 5.6 miles, then turn right on Road 93. This one-lane road with turnouts is actively used by logging trucks, so be careful. Follow it 13 miles. At the junction with Road 9327, veer right to stay on Road 93. In another mile, turn right on Road 9328. You'll find a large gravel parking area in 0.1 mile.

Elevation: 3,700 feet

Campsites: No campsites, just parking for many trailers on a large, flat, graveled area surrounded by trees suitable for high-lining.

Facilities: None. No toilet, no picnic tables, no fire pits, no corrals.

Permits: None

Season: Summer through fall

Contact: Mt. Adams Ranger District, 509-395-3400

Wright Meadow Area Trails

Trail	Difficulty	Elevation	Round Trip
Blue Lake Loop	Moderate	3,500-4,600	11 miles
Craggy Peak Trail	Challenging	3,500-5,300	14 miles
Lewis River Waterfalls	Challenging	3,650-1,550	10-13 miles
Wright Meadow Loop	Moderate	3,500-3,750	5.5 miles

Blue Lake Loop

Trailhead:	Start at Wright Meadow primitive camp
Length:	11 miles round trip
Elevation:	3,500 to 4,600 feet
Difficulty:	Moderate -- some steep side hills, trail is deeply rutted in places, possible motorcycle traffic
Footing:	Hoof protection recommended
Season:	Summer through fall
Permits:	None
Facilities:	None. Stock water is available on the trail.

Highlights: This delightful loop takes you up along Wright Creek, through dense old-growth forest, through lighter woods with huckleberries and bear grass, and on to the aptly-named Blue Lake. This sapphire gem is nestled at the base of a rock face and is a great spot for lunch. The return route offers easy traveling as it mostly follows gravel roads.

The Ride: Begin by following one of the old forest roads that head eastward from the camping area, and in about 100 feet you'll reach

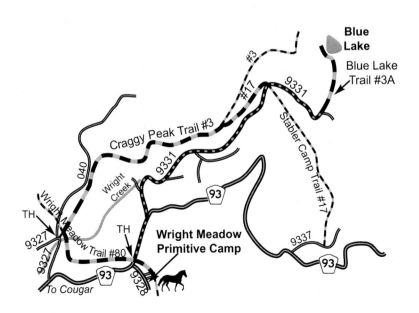

the Wright Meadow Trail #80. Turn left on it, and in 0.3 mile the trail crosses Road 93 at a trailhead. After another 0.9 mile it reaches an unsigned 4-way junction. Turn right here and you'll be on the Craggy Peak Trail #3. The trail runs though a tree plantation on the side hill above Wright Creek for the next 0.7 mile, then the terrain levels out and the trail enters a stretch of dense old-growth forest. In another 1.9 miles you'll reach the junction with the Stabler Camp Trail #17. Turn right here, and in 0.6 mile the trail crosses gravel Road 9331. Turn left on Road 9331 and follow it for 0.9 mile. Where the road forks, go to the left and in 200 feet the road ends and the single-track Blue Lake Trail #3A begins. Follow the trail for 0.6 mile to reach the shore of beautiful Blue Lake. For your return journey, ride back to Road 9331 and follow it, this time for 3.2 miles, to its intersection with Road 93. Turn right here and in 0.5 mile turn left on either the Wright Meadow Trail or Road 9328 to return to your trailer.

Shelley on Johnnie Walker and Donna on Star,
giving the horses a well-deserved drink at pretty Blue Lake.

Craggy Peak Trail

Trailhead: Start at Wright Meadow primitive camp

Length: 14 miles round trip

Elevation: 3,500 to 5,300 feet

Difficulty: Challenging -- some steep side hills, deeply rutted trail, significant elevation change, and possible motorcycle traffic

Footing: Hoof protection suggested

Season: Summer through fall

Permits: None

Facilities: None. Stock water is available on the trail.

Highlights: If you want stunning mountain views and beautiful wild flowers in season, this is the trail for you. In return, you'll have to cope with a few steep side hills and a trail that is deeply rutted in places by motorcycle traffic. There are several places along this trail where you wouldn't want to meet a motorcycle, so use caution.

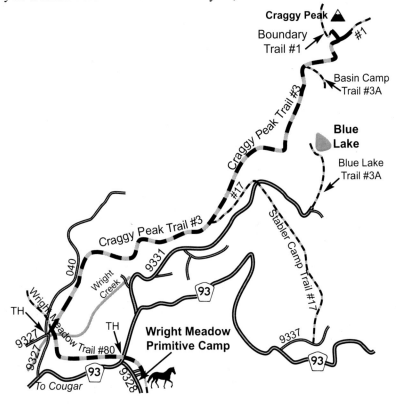

Donna and Shelley ride Star and Johnnie Walker
toward Craggy Peak.

The Ride: Begin by following one of the old forest roads that head eastward from the camping area, and in about 100 feet you'll reach the Wright Meadow Trail #80. Turn left on it, and in 0.3 mile the trail crosses Road 93 at a trailhead, then in another 0.9 mile it crosses Wright Creek and comes to an unsigned 4-way junction. Turn right here and you'll be on the Craggy Peak Trail #3. Follow it across the side hill above Wright Creek, through some dense old-growth forest, and through younger forest with an understory of bear grass and huckleberries. After 2.6 miles you'll pass the junction with the Stabler Camp Trail #17 on the right. Stay left, and for much of the next 2.4 miles you'll be climbing the side of a steep ridge. You'll be rewarded with views of Mt. St. Helens, Mt. Hood, Mt. Adams, and Mt. Rainier. Plus you'll be treated to a wildflower extravaganza -- depending on the season you'll see oceans of bear grass, lupine, corn lilies, and much more. When you come to the junction with the Basin Camp Trail #3A on the right, again stay left. (This extremely steep trail goes down to a pretty little meadow in the basin below, but the trail is badly eroded and is not horse friendly. And the trail beyond the basin has not been maintained and is impassible. Don't go there.) In 0.7 mile beyond this junction you'll reach the Boundary Trail #1. If you turn left and ride 0.1 mile you'll be treated to great views of Mt. Rainier and Shark Rock. If you turn right and ride 0.2 mile, you'll see wildflower meadows stretching up toward the summit of Craggy Peak and down into Straight Creek Basin. Retrace your steps to return to your trailer.

Lewis River Waterfalls

Trailhead: Start at Wright Meadow primitive camp

Length: 10 miles round trip to Middle Falls, or 13 miles round trip to Lower Falls

Elevation: 3,650 to 1,650 feet to Middle Falls, or 3,650 to 1,550 feet to Lower Falls

Difficulty: Challenging -- very steep and rutted trail, big elevation change, and possible motorcycle traffic

Footing: Hoof protection suggested

Season: Summer through fall

Permits: None

Facilities: None. Stock water is available on the trail.

Highlights: This is a strenuous ride, with an 1,800-foot elevation loss/gain in 3 miles. The trail is rutted by motorcycle traffic and erosion so your horse will have to contend with large step-ups/step-downs

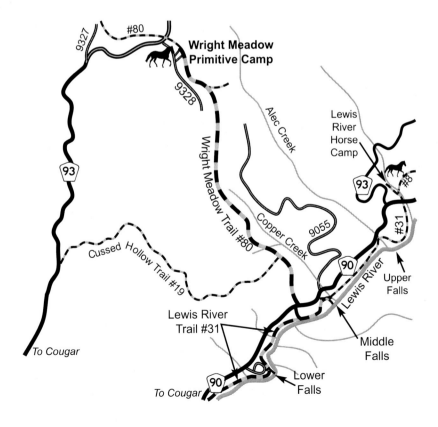

over roots. But if your horse is sure-footed and in good condition this ride will give you a great view of Mt. Adams and spectacular views of the falls on the Lewis River. When we were researching this book, the Lewis River Trail was closed to stock because several bridges had washed out. So once we came to Road 90 we turned and rode beside it to reach the parking areas and access the trails to the falls.

The Ride: Begin by following one of the old forest roads that head eastward from the primitive camping area, and in about 100 feet you'll reach the Wright Meadow Trail #80. Turn right on it, and in 0.7 mile an unsigned trail will go off to the left. Continue straight on the Wright Meadow Trail. In 1.3 miles you'll cross a tributary of Copper Creek. In another 0.3 mile the Cussed Hollow Trail #19 goes off to the right, and 0.8 mile after that you'll reach paved Road 90. If the bridges have been repaired, you can ride across the road and in 100 feet turn right on the Lewis River Trail #31 to head to Lower Falls or left to go to Middle Falls. If the bridges are still out, you can follow Road 90 to the parking areas for each of these falls and ride the short access trails that will take you to the waterfalls. Retrace your steps to return to your trailer.

Middle Lewis River Falls

Wright Meadow Loop

Trailhead: Start at Wright Meadow primitive camp
Length: 5.5 miles round trip
Elevation: 3,500 to 3,750 feet
Difficulty: Moderate -- bridge, possible creek ford, deeply rutted trail
Footing: Hoof protection recommended
Season: Summer through fall
Permits: None
Facilities: None. Stock water is available on the trail.

Highlights: This pleasant lollipop loop circles Wright Meadow, though you will only occasionally glimpse the meadow through the trees as you ride along its eastern edge. The return leg of the loop follows lightly-graveled Road 9327 and has no views of the meadow. However, it's a nice orientation ride to acquaint you with the trails in this area.

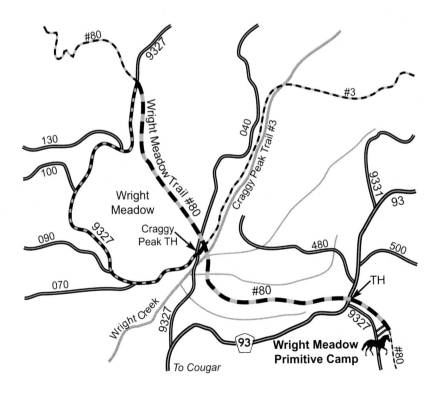

Shelley on Johnnie Walker and Donna on Star,
traveling along the Wright Meadow Trail.

The Ride: The Wright Meadow Trail #80 runs through the forest just east of the primitive camping area. Follow one of the old forest roads that head eastward and in about 100 feet you'll reach the Wright Meadow Trail. Turn left on it, and in 0.2 mile the trail crosses Road 93 at a trailhead. In another 0.9 mile you'll cross Wright Creek and come to a 4-way junction. Go straight ahead on the Wright Meadow Trail. You'll soon pass Wright Meadow on your right, though you'll only catch occasional glimpses of the meadow through the forest. In another mile the trail crosses Road 9327. From here the trail heads downhill, losing about 1,000 feet of elevation in 2 miles before climbing again and ending at Road 101. You can ride out as far as you like, or turn left on Road 9327 for an easy jaunt back to the Craggy Peak Trailhead in 1.9 miles. (The trailhead is tucked back in the trees just off Road 9327.) Pick up the Craggy Peak Trail and at the 4-way junction in 100 feet turn right on the Wright Meadow Trail to return to your trailer.

Lupine

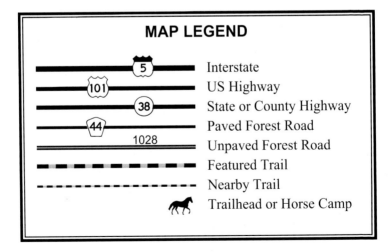

Index

Upper Elk Spur Trail, near Sahara Creek Horse Camp.

Happy trails to you, until we meet again.

Dale Evans Rogers